THE GERMAN NOVEL, 1939-1944

H. BOESCHENSTEIN

The German Novel, 1939-1944

UNIVERSITY OF TORONTO PRESS, 1949

Preface

A REPORT such as this could be undertaken with only one legitimate objective: to sort out, or to begin sorting out, for the benefit of future historians of literature, the large number of German literary works which the war has piled up before us. I have tried to do just this with whatever novels were obtainable. I hope that by culling the chaff away I have saved others from wasting their time on it, and that by indicating the content of the more significant novels, and to a less degree their stylistic characteristics, I have shortened the task of future research.

Even though keeping this practical aim constantly in mind, it was yet impossible to go on reading without an intense personal curiosity. Would these books confirm the widely held conviction that German publishers brought out nothing but trash during the last fifteen years? Or would they prove that F. A. Voigt, the editor of the *Nineteenth Century,* knew what he was talking about when, during the war, he hinted that the standard of literary and critical production in contemporary France and Germany was remarkably high?[1]

It appears that Mr. Voigt was right, if the limited scope of this investigation provides a fair indication also of what was done in the drama and the lyric, and in the adjacent field of philosophical writing. Now, if the readers of the *Nineteenth Century* could be warned, even during the strain of those war years, not to think too lightly of the current intellectual and spiritual efforts of their enemies, then surely students of literature should by now be in a sufficiently intelligent and tolerant mood to accept some detailed evidence and to begin to scrutinize it objectively.

[1]"France and Germany," *Nineteenth Century And After,* CXXXII (1942), 241-51.

Needless to say, a more competent judgment, to say nothing of a final verdict, can only be formed when more reports are received on the field covered here, and especially on those vast areas which had to be left out of consideration. Apart from a few articles on individual books we have, so far, only one brief outline of recent German writing. In *Pens under the Swastika,* W. W. Schütz, in addition to critical and scholarly works, also examines German books that were published outside of the Reich.[1] Neither of these fields has been considered in the present survey. As far as the number of novels accessible for investigation is concerned I seem to have had more luck than Mr. Schütz. Even so he mentions a few titles which I should have liked to include had they but come to my attention—a strong reminder that it will be some time before anything like an exhaustive survey can be attempted and a more definitive opinion be stated.

The opportunity to acquire and to look into a considerable volume of German literary works published during the war came to me in my capacity as Director of the War Prisoners' Aid of the Y.M.C.A., when I was visiting POW camps in Canada, from 1943 to 1946. Recollection of those years will always dwell with a feeling of deep appreciation upon the assistance I received from Colonel H. N. Streight, Lt. Colonel H. W. Pearson, and Mr. Tracy Strong. In facilitating my work in general they enabled me to devote some of my time to academic interests.

A most direct and more than usual debt of gratitude I owe, however, to Miss F. G. Halpenny, Assistant Editor of the University of Toronto Press, whose help in the preparation of the manuscript proved invaluable.

A list of the novels published in Grossdeutschland between 1939 and 1944 which I was able to secure will be found in the Bibliography, with their dates of publication. Dates of critical and scholarly works and of novels that appeared prior to 1939 are indicated in the text.

H. B.

[1]*Pens under the Swastika: A Study in Recent German Writing* (London, 1946).

Contents

THE GERMAN NOVEL, 1939-1944

1 Form and Content

WHAT interest recent German novels may arouse stems rather from their content than from their form. With very few exceptions they follow traditional methods and techniques, and use a style that has a familiar ring. For notwithstanding many claims to the contrary, National Socialism was not accompanied or supported by a vigorous literary movement. Blood and soil literature is in content merely the offshoot of an older regional naturalism; still less did the political upheaval create a literary style of its own. That a number of authors were experimenting with untraditional techniques will be readily conceded. This cannot compensate for the master-shots that were never fired. Recent German novelists, of the lesser kind, are by and large working in a singularly spiceless linguistic medium. This disadvantage becomes glaringly evident when we compare their language with that of modern Anglo-Saxon and especially modern American fiction, where a raciness of diction, a freshness of dialogue create the impression of something new and produce a story that arrests our attention even when the new linguistic weave is used for traditional content patterns. In contrast with the style of American fiction, German diction, too often a fabric of clichés, looks faded, washed out. This condition of tepid listlessness cannot possibly be attributed to accident, that is, to the fact that no great word artist or language creator has appeared on the German scene in the last few years. It is not the absence of personal linguistic virtuosity which is to be deplored, but the lack of contact with lively language. Such language is never the creation of one man only, or of a few men; it develops from a healthy emotional, intellectual, and occupational group life, from a richly integrated society that is free to air all its concerns frankly.

If there is a possible exception to this rule of linguistic sterility it is a novel by Maximilian Böttcher, *Krach im Vorderhaus*— and it only tends to prove the rule. Here an author for once dares to speak the language of the people, of a group that has long been noted for native wit and indigenous linguistic vitality, the Berliners. The story, a love story in which a lower middle-class family is brought close to, and then again separated from, the upper-class milieu of a lawyer, releases all the idiomatic reserves of the local vernacular and the slang of Berlin tenement houses; the plot, interesting as it is, serves mainly as the channel for an incessant flow of language. A few political discussions, conforming strictly to official standards, may mar but cannot spoil the impression of this novel, whose substance is contained in its language rather than in any social and political attitudes evolved in the course of its events. To read this book and to follow the never ending conversations carried on by common people, enriched by their native intellectual acumen and emotional vivacity, is to forget for a few happy hours the existence of that official jargon which all but paralysed the German language. That Böttcher was able to ignore this jargon and to replenish his vocabulary and syntax from the source of unsophisticated speech, goes far to show that linguistic naturalness and common sense, and all that these stand for, are as much alive as ever and that what is needed is the courage to tap these invigorating springs.

Many recent German authors, even those of considerable merit, preferred to leave the resources of native thought and dialect language unused and to withdraw, instead, into traditional styles. Hence the impression of a number of successful imitations of stylistic traditions which, just because they are good imitations, strike one as excessively impersonal and timid. Too often this studied emulation of an earlier novelist results in the assimilation of static mannerisms rather than in the recovery of the spiritual matrix. Wilhelm Raabe's style, for instance—the whimsical encircling of a thought or of a character, the skill, developed almost to a fault, in pulling the wires of his marionettes and in keeping up a constant communication with them, even while they are talking with one another and not with the author—has found good copyists in Kurt Kluge and others. But there is little evidence of Raabe's serenity and wisdom, except perhaps in Kluge who succeeds in being witty and in producing a satirical illumination of human nature, notably in *Die Zaubergeige*.

Theodor Fontane, on the other hand, with whom some German writers have always felt immediate affinities, penetrated into deeper levels of creative writing. It would be difficult for a German novelist writing about Berlin or about the Berlin environment not to follow in the paths marked out by Fontane, if only because it is difficult to experience life in Brandenburg in any other way than through the medium of his novels. The spirit of his philosophy, even if one could avoid drawing it into oneself from the primary source, his novels, seems to have become diffused in the course of time into the very air of Brandenburg. While we may never again see the whole of this world contained in one novel, or in a series of novels, as it is in Fontane—the Berlin servants and coachmen; the middle class with its teachers, bankers, doctors, lawyers, and civil servants; the junkers of the old estates—we are bound to encounter large fragments of Fontane's humanity in novels dealing with Berlin and its environment. The lower classes in Böttcher's *Krach im Vorderhaus*, the upper strata in the two monumental volumes of von Simpson's generation novel of the Barrings,[1] and the middle layers in Fechter's *Der Herr Ober* all seem to have their ancestors in the work of Fontane. This is a tradition that deserves to be cultivated: when applied to the lower social levels it discovers there a rare common sense, exhilarating humour, and deeply felt human sympathies; on the higher levels, where discussion of and contact with politics, art, and science are involved, the Fontane tradition guarantees a degree of *Weltoffenheit* and a standard of social decorum that establish a strong bond between Germany and Western ideals of tolerance, intelligence, and serenity.

Of the many German novelists continuing in the Fontane

[1]William von Simpson, *Die Barrings* (1937), and its continuation, *Der Enkel*.

tradition, William von Simpson is the most gifted. In more than one respect he has assumed Fontane's task of analysing the social and political life of the Prussian junkers. Taking up the thread in Bismarck's time, when Germany appeared strongest, he follows the story to its bitter end, regretfully but mercilessly, using the fate of an East Prussian landowning family, the Barrings, to exemplify and symbolize the decline of Imperial Germany. Some of the main causes of the decline are revealed in the young Emperor William, himself only talented and not a genius, and surrounded by counsellors lacking in wisdom; in the disregard into which Bismarck and his policy are allowed to fall; in a nobility that is in a state of progressive petrifaction and has lost its sense of responsibility towards the nation as a whole; in a military clique that is more concerned with the code of honour than with professional efficiency. To be sure, the grandson of old Barring learns from all these mistakes and shortcomings the necessity of a fresh start attuned to more democratic ideals; but the conversion comes too late and will save neither the family nor the nation. The War of 1914, for which this last scion of the Barrings departs at the end of the second volume, will seal the doom of the era. Within this framework of intelligent reflection on the inevitably tragic course of German history after Bismarck's death, the author gives full scope to the Fontane tradition in his use of descriptive detail, in the balance of serenity with deep apprehension, and, best of all, in the advocacy, to the very last, of genuine humanism. As Fontane tried, so does von Simpson try once more to bring the English way of life to the sympathetic attention of his German countrymen, to bridge the gap of mis-understandings, though he ominously senses the futility of his effort. Comparisons between von Simpson's novel of the Barrings with Thomas Mann's *Buddenbrooks* will no doubt be forthcoming in due time; it should not be difficult to work out the different conception underlying the treatment of the process of decadence in the two families. In some respects, von Simpson's character-ization of a dying period is much less pessimistic than Thomas Mann's, as he sees no validity in a parallelism between biological

[6]

decline and artistic, intellectual vigour. Physically, the older Barring towers high above his peers among the nobility of East Prussia, and also above his son and his grandson; at the same time he is a man of true culture, well informed, intellectually alert, and considerate of others. He is married to a former dancer (a counterpart to Gerda, the wife of Thomas Buddenbrooks) but nowhere does the author insinuate that connexion with the world of art has had a weakening effect on the Barrings. In fact no doubt is left that old Barring owes much of his refined vitality to his wife. The decline of the family, and of the nation in general, results, in the final analysis, from a weakening social coherence which in turn can be traced to a lack of genuine intellectual and spiritual effort and not, as Thomas Mann would have us believe, to the inactivating influence of culture.

It is only natural to seek reasons why Raabe and Fontane have remained favoured models for German novelists. Can it be because both offer a way of escape from the tense, hoarse diction so characteristic of the official jargon? Raabe's ironic turns, by which he manages to be now very close to and now again at a critical distance from his objects; Fontane's absorption in detail, his inconspicuous observance of all rules for good story-telling, and his mellowed attitude to life—both styles would attract writers who, in order to save their self-respect without forfeiting the right to publish, were in search of a stylistic refuge. Perhaps, too, they saw here the opportunity for an occasional stab at officialdom, under the disguise of Raabe's irony or Fontane's seemingly impersonal objectivity.

Such an explanation ties in with the fact that there are other stylistic media to be observed in recent German writing which might also have aided in the escape from popular prose styles.

The first of these media is a diction that lies somewhere between the realistic and the classical—terse, succinct, close to the object and therefore absorbed by it, so that the temptation to make subjective digressions is reduced to a minimum. Where this style occurs in conjunction with a classical theme, or with a modern theme set in the classical world or in a kind of literary no man's land, it renders perfect service to writers who need the support of a respectable tradition in a time that has not produced a literary style of its own. Hermann Stahl (*Die Heimkehr des Odysseus*), Paul Gurk (*Iskander*), Hans Sassmann (*Xanthippe*), have ostentatiously moved away into antiquity; others like Werner Helwig (*Raubfischer in Hellas*), Emil Barth (*Das Lorbeerufer*), Marianne Langewiesche (*Die Allerheiligen Bucht*), hover in the vicinity of classical territory though they deal with modern problems; and yet, take away a few chronological hints and the stories are set free in timelessness.[1]

By making this objective, non-committal style even more impersonal and factual, and by applying it to and developing it on the subject-matter of hard, dry facts, recent German writers have perfected another variety of diction, issuing in a brittle, realistic presentation of factual knowledge which often assumes the terse appearance of reporting. In *Das tönende Licht,* Guido Bagier emphasizes in an explanatory note this aim at concreteness: "The [book is a] description of strange occurrences that have happened since the invention of cinematography, compiled with the aid of important and hitherto unknown documents." It is not quite clear what the author means by "unknown documents." The bibliography added to his novel mentions no fewer than ninety-seven authors and many more works, and one would think that these would contain all the information needed to dramatize the coming into life of the moving pictures and the talkies.

K. A. Schenzinger developed this realistic chronicle style to a point where it refused to serve fiction and reverted to its more proper function of recording cold facts in as few words as possible. Both in *Anilin* (1937) and in *Metall* he places before and sometimes even intersperses in his narrative chapters (each of which, in the case of *Metall,* features some memorable event in the history of the discovery, utilization, and exploitation of the various

[1]A curious experiment was made by Erich August Mayer in a novel called *Paulusmarkt 17*, in which he describes post-war life in a small Austrian town in classical hexameters. In spite of its great metrical skill the novel would have lost nothing if it had been written in prose. First published in 1935, the book was reprinted in 1943.

metals) some brief resumé such as this: "The human eye is like a camera. The film is for the camera what the retina is for the eye: the light-sensitive part. Just as we have silver granules on a film, so in the sensitive layer of the retina we find the end-cells of the nerves of light. The nerve of sight has a diameter of two millimetres. . . ." And so the matter-of-fact report continues, leading on to the history of the first cinematographic inventions. It is in a style attuned to the requirements of historical accuracy: no amount of fictitious embellishment can deceive us as to the basically objective and wholly unimaginative character of this kind of diction and composition; at best, imagination functions here as a kind of applied art, not as a creative force.

Franz Kafka is rightly regarded as having worked at the opposite pole from descriptive realism, with an autonomous imagination that follows its own laws. During the years of National Socialism, German writers were hardly in a position to acknowledge indebtedness to a writer whose works were officially denounced as decadent and *artfremd*. Yet Fritz Nölle's *Herrn Kesperleins seltsame Reise* and, to a lesser extent, Hans Ewers' *Kilian Menkes Veränderung* belong to all intents and purposes to the Kafka tradition, if the word may be applied to this literary style in which precise narration drives its shaft into the magic mountain of sovereign imagination. On second thought one wonders why more writers have not followed this vein which, in yielding a dreamlike reality, affords ample opportunities to release suppressed emotions and ideas, consciously and, if necessary, maliciously. Herr Kesperlein who all of a sudden decides, in middle age, to leave his hardware business and to set out on a journey ("something in his successful life, nay in the character of the whole period struck him as being all wrong and in need of correction; some of his inner forces had been suppressed and were now apparently spreading their wings") may seem erratic, a fool in many ways, though he is a wise fool at times, and, if the author had cared to make him so, could have been wiser still. Even so Nölle manages to say very definite things about the stupidity of mankind—in its distant origin simple and pure, but

[9]

now governed by the blind desire to amass riches. Ewers' novel, a detective story, in which an innocent fellow is abducted and forced to remain near the scene of a jewel theft in order that his resemblance to one of the criminals may attract the attention of the police, makes, to be sure, no satirical sorties such as Nölle's; but as a piece of truly imaginative fiction the yarn brings welcome relief from a fact-ridden literary world.

The projection of sharply conceived characters into the mystery of a boldly created world requires imagination of the highest order. But merely to inject mystery into ordinary occurrences is a cheap trick and a matter of mannerism. *Die Gesellschaft der Jugend,* by Franz Dietz, purports to rewrite the history of the post-war generation—its perversity, strained parental relations, abortions, and shady speculations in American dollars—in the style of "magic realism." But the author masters only the pseudo-magic practice of lifting a veil bit by bit, without ever revealing any secrets behind it, or of first asking a dozen questions and then giving the simple answer; it is as if all the many characters were made to walk backward to a goal which the reader perceives clearly all the while, and which they might reach much faster by normal steps. This style has as little to do with Kafka's as have the mannerisms of Jakob Wassermann, whose technique undergoes an undesirable revival in Dietz's novel.

The great danger in relaxing formal and stylistic exertions is that too much reliance comes to be placed on the interest which the content, plot, and characters of a novel are expected to produce in the reader. Young novelists are almost invariably carried away by their confidence in the startling novelty of their message. As they see it, they bring to our attention matters of such import that there is no special need to narrate them well; not infrequently a false sense of modesty or honesty bids them spurn technical considerations which they dismiss as an unworthy *captatio benevolentiae*. It is obvious that large sections of recent German fiction have suffered from such neglect of form. Novelists who tell in a simple, straightforward manner of their participation in the political life of a turbulent period, or record their own experience in one or two world wars, may be treated with a degree of leniency. It is, however, a different matter when many writers of peasant novels, of blood and soil literature, take it for granted that our delight in haymaking or the doing of chores is such as to make the slightest artistic exertion superfluous, or even suspicious. Yet this is, with few exceptions, what has happened—with the result that scores of German novels are outside the range of literature. However, a few writers took advantage of this situation, of this boring artlessness that must have driven the more sophisticated reader to the skilful novelists of former days, and concentrated on achieving technical perfection, determined to continue a tradition which in pre-war days was exemplified by the consummate skill of writers like Schnitzler, Ponten, and, in a lesser measure, Wilhelm Schäfer. In consequence there are a number of novels which, though light in their philosophical weight, deploy all the dexterities of good story-telling and captivate us by means of their formal brilliance, no matter how ancient some of their virtuoso tricks may be. The amorous scenes in *Boemo Divino* by Carl von Pidoll, especially, are in the best tradition of European narrative art; *Stechinelli*, by Werner von der Schulenburg, the story of an Italian noble transplanted to the court of Lüneburg, in the second half of the seventeenth century, can stand comparison with that singular combination of apt psychological analysis, lucid presentation, and firm dramatic structure to which Somerset Maugham invariably treats his readers.

Striking changes in novelistic technique are not something invented by a resourceful craftsman in his workshop. They originate as a result of, or simultaneously with, a new personal or collective apprehension of reality and involve a novel experience of time, space, and human character. As far as can be seen, there is no evidence that there took place in Germany the kind of refreshing re-experience which could have compelled startling technical changes in the novel—or in any other literary genre for that matter. Nor was the time propitious for the assimilation of new modes of experience as they appeared in some foreign novelists.

For instance, we do not see even a timid emulation of the stream of consciousness technique which for a few years did so much, outside Germany, to render the study of the novel a stimulating intellectual enterprise. Alfred Döblin's *Berlin Alexanderplatz* (1928) remains the one and only major attempt in this direction. Since there was no irresistible inner force at work creating a new style in diction and composition, it is no surprise to find a formal eclecticism in which all the traditional elements meet.

This use of long-established forms does not, of course, preclude excursions into hitherto neglected or unconquered realms of life, or at any rate into such new material aspects of civilization as do not perceptibly modify the texture of human relationships.

Sports and technical inventions loom large in this intake of new factual material: they form attractive ingredients in many a conventional plot. Their novelty as raw material has by now sufficiently worn off that they no longer monopolize the attention of the reader to the extent that the plot appears negligible. *Flugschüler Ungenat*, by Hans Wörner, one of the few novels taking us into World War II, is set against the background of an air training school and tries successfully to relegate this novel subject-matter to a subordinate place in order to leave room for a love story. The prize, however, for the complete leavening of modern, technical raw material must go to Hans Rabl for his novel *Das Ziel in den Wolken* (1937), which features the first appearance, in Germany, of Orville Wright, and the eager competition of a few German tyros in the art of flying. Such integration of new technical implements into literature is a continuous task: railways and bicycles, automobiles and aeroplanes have all had to be made manageable for artistic treatment; the process must be repeated with more recent inventions. It is an almost automatic process, and one which does not call for unusual sensibilities.

In contrast with these mechanical gadgets that civilization tosses into the lap of art, there are the marginal provinces of human existence which have to be explored, or changes in the social fabric which the novelist must try to understand. One has but to think of the slow conquest of proletarian levels of life by literature, to realize how much more difficult it is to adjust artistic sensibilities to such new human interests than it is to apprehend merely material changes.

What is really only a minor gain should nevertheless be mentioned in connexion with this expansion of human sympathy and understanding. When writing *Der Herr Ober,* a sortie, as it were, into the world of a Berlin waiter, Paul Fechter may not have been conscious of pushing the boundaries of novelistic material further; yet in his story the waiter for the first time leaves his time-honoured position in the background and steps into the limelight of literary presentation. The author does not make any effort to stress the novelty of his subject-matter.[1] The accent is on the love affair of the hero, a belated infatuation of a married man which ends with his elegiac-serene return to his wife, a wiser man come back to a wise, plucky woman. What insight we receive into the occupational sphere of waiters comes quite unobtrusively and casually, in the course of the events. Yet though this presentation of life as seen through the eyes of the man who runs back and forth from the kitchen to the guests' table is quietly woven into the plot, it makes a most definite impression since it is the fruit of long and intimate observation. The presentation of such observation is an important service that literature can render, and no less gratifying because the object of these new sensibilities is "only" a waiter. Rather does the latter fact enhance the significance of the event, acquainting us, as it does, with a trade which most people expect to have at their beck and call without knowing much about its psychology.

The fact that Fechter made a lone excursion into new territory does not, of course, affect my prediction that recent German novels will be read for their content and not for their stylistic qualities, even if the latter should on occasion be found to be more pronounced than these introductory remarks indicate. It is only natural to be curious with regard to the topics in which the

[1]Arthur Berkun, on the other hand, in *Kamerad Bursche* rants about his intention to erect a monument to those forgotten "pillars and girders of the German Imperial Army," the batmen. The result is a string of sentimental incidents spiced with a crude brand of humour.

Germans were interested, or were expected to be interested, under National Socialism. The degree of deviation from, or co-ordination with, the interests of the Western or Eastern world has, after all, some bearing on current problems of reconstruction. An attempt will therefore be made in the following chapters to circumscribe such spheres of interest and such fundamental moods as were obviously either eagerly studied or signally neglected by German novelists.

2 Peasant Life

THERE seems to have been no relief, during the war years, from the continuous output of peasant novels; numerically the genre far outdistances even historical fiction. Whether this excessive production of blood and soil literature was in response to an equally great demand on the part of readers, is doubtful, in view of the fact that this kind of fiction has long been available in large quantities. For since the pattern is not greatly influenced by time, most of the older peasant novels serve the purpose just as well as recent ones.

One of the reasons why so many novelists choose their themes from amongst the rural inhabitants is the safety factor. No matter how badly you write or how inaccurately you observe, as long as you sing the praise of country life the critics will have to credit you at least with a wholesome, biologically valuable philosophy.

There were other, contributary reasons for this swelling flow of peasant novels. For instance, genuine regionalists, writing as always close to the soil, did not need to change their subject, simply because it was being appropriated by inept outsiders. On the contrary, they had every reason to continue a tradition which all of a sudden had been lifted from a secondary position to that of a representative movement. Again, to Catholic writers, especially those of Bavaria and Austria, the blood and soil vogue must have seemed a useful expedient, for, by making their religious beliefs part of its scheme of realistic narrative, they could protect them. All they had to do was to underline the Catholic lore inherent in the peasant life of their provinces. This was one way in which they could render unto Caesar what was due him, and yet preserve their greater loyalty to God. Their ingenuity in grafting new political slogans upon the old religious tradition, or vice versa, is, on occasion, remarkable.

A few of these many writers had a relevant contribution to make to the literary discussion of farm and village life; far from glorifying everything that goes on in the mind of a *Hofbauer* they observed critically and described rural conditions unsparingly, if not sarcastically. While the opportunity to produce a modern Don Quixote of the *"Erbhof"* seems to have been allowed to pass by unused, there are at least indications of a sober approach to rural sociology.

Out of a number of patterns to which all peasant novels conform, two seem to be the special product of a kind of brutal sentimentality for which everything that happens on the farm is right.

The simpler of these patterns is that of a biographical portrait of some young fellow who has his *Erbhof* waiting for him and who therefore lives under the protection of an unwritten law decreeing that whatever such a *Jungbauer* does is acceptable, by virtue of the sacrosanct guild he will sooner or later belong to. No matter how often he runs foul of the game warden, or of the village police, and regardless of the plight of some unfortunate servant girl who may bear his child, the boy in his leather shorts and green hat always emerges a smiling, whistling child of nature. He exists outside the pale of ordinary laws as long as he remains faithful to his one calling, which is to inherit the farm when the time comes, and to work on it until his own oldest or youngest boy will in turn take over from him. Curt Strohmeyer presents this type of biography in *Mein silbergrauer Weggefährte*. The hero owns a silver-grey rifle that accompanies him through life, in peace and in war, as the symbol of complete independence and as the indispensable complement to that other basic tool of the farmer, the silver-grey plough. If you have these two, and if you know when to use them, you do not need to worry. You can go through life without fear of law-enforcing bureaucrats or of law-defying social democrats. This is as good a book as the Hermann Löns tradition could have produced, and as naïvely brutal in its praise of untroubled egotism as anything the blood and soil movement has brought forth.

The second of these patterns, that of the saga, if it does not claim that the farmer is always right, takes at any rate for granted that whatever you jot down about farm life will make interesting reading. Hence the monotonous juxtaposition of all and sundry that goes on in the country, harvest dances and incendiary fires, rainstorms and bread-baking. There is no emphasis, and no selection except that imposed by limited supplies of paper.[1] Even with this limitation the saga producers rake together a pile of hay that requires for its assimilation a more than human digestive system. That a publishing house with the reputation of Eugen Diederichs should have taken the chief exponent of the saga pattern, Joseph Georg Oberkofler, under its wing, comes as a shock. For both *Der Bannwald* and *Die Flachsbraut* repeat with the monotony of a hurdy-gurdy the old story that the clan is more important than the individual member of it, and the farm of greater consequence than the farmer. If proof is needed that the old Icelandic saga is best left alone and cannot support a literary renaissance, *Die Flachsbraut* will furnish it, with its conjured-up concoction of Nordic fogs and Scandinavian proper names, and with a German syntax that makes the gnawing of a porcupine sound melodious.

By comparison, every other peasant novel pattern looks exciting. One such pattern, centring on the theme of the road back from the city to the land, offers indeed rich possibilities for an interesting fabric wrought out of the sinful episodes of city life; indulgence in moral laxity may be freely practised, since the hero, in the end, will ruefully return to the farm.

"It is too bad that so much rich soil lies buried under a city"— this is the motto Hans Wörner gives his novel *Der Weg durch die Stadt.* As the title indicates, the hero, initially a good-natured farmhand, does not stay forever in the city into which a renegade village girl had lured him. The glitter of cheap amusements fades away. Luck is with the simple fellow; he is invited to accompany

---

[1] *Der Erdgeist,* by Hermann Eris Busse, is not a saga in spite of its subtitle, *Saga vom Oberrhein,* but a wonderfully rich picture of the Hegau district; it is one of the finest German regional novels.

a veterinary doctor into a border province ravaged by the hoof and mouth disease. His assistance to a once wealthy farmer, whose livestock had to be slain, is duly rewarded with the love of the farmer's beautiful daughter. In another novel (*König am Jykän*) which does not so definitely belong to this genre, Wörner is much less critical of city life and much more just to the problems encountered therein, an indication, it would seem, of the irresponsibility with which a black and white contrast between city and country life is being used and sentimentalized by Wörner and others to suit the purpose of blood and soil literature.

Kurd Schulz in *Michael Conrad* provides no happy solution for the son of a well-to-do Pomeranian farmer who moves into town, again under the influence of a pleasure-loving woman. In addition to ruining his own life Hans Fried Conrad brings the whole *Erbhof* tumbling down, and the children of what was once a widely known and respected family have to emigrate to America.

Ernst Wurm in *Der Bürger* may not have succeeded in proving what he set out to demonstrate: that city life has reached a critical stage which requires nothing less than a complete rebirth of man. Yet his description of a comfortably situated *bourgeois* innocently experiencing all the social disgrace that life can pile upon him, including an ill-advised second marriage and a rotter of a son who sleeps with his stepmother, assumes an almost classical grandeur. Instead of admitting defeat and breaking under the blows of fate the hero, well on in his sixties, rallies his last strength and sets out reborn and rejuvenated with the few worldly possessions he still has, to start from scratch as a settler clearing a plot of waste land. "He half stretched his arms away from him with the gesture of Christ freeing himself from the darkness of his grave." Like a strong Christ, the author hastens to add, not like the Christs of the crossroad images with their distastefully thin bodies. The religious meaning read into man's striving away from city life to regain regenerative forces, attests to the Catholic origin of the novel, while its setting around Wiener Neustadt points to its Austrian nativity.

Another group of peasant novels, perhaps the largest in number, has as its main theme the preservation of the farm, its rescue from the hands of the inept or unworthy possessor; this is often accomplished by the miraculous appearance, in the eleventh hour, of a saviour—a son, for instance, returning from a long, adventurous interlude of soldiering (Hans Heitmann, *Die Flut*; Josefa Berens-Totenohl, *Der Fels*). The pattern in question allows of a particularly popular variation: the farm passes over into the possession of a daughter who may or may not have the right idea for choosing a husband (Walter Sperling, *Wassernächte*; Rudolf Ahlers, *Das weite Land*; Luise Westkirch, *Der Hof im Moor*; and others).

It was inevitable that blood and soil writers would not forever be content with the traditional role of the farmer as a paragon of healthy living and vital thinking, but would have to extol his inestimable services in the preservation and defence of Germandom. Since it would hardly be fair to take the farmer away from the soil and turn him into a political busy-body neglecting his chores, a more silent yet very important task was assigned to him, the protection of German border districts against the infiltration of foreign elements or against the encroachment of some non-Germanic majority. For instance, Paul Seelhoff (*Acker und Steine*) tells of the watch German farmers kept along the Danish border before 1864; Otto Boris (*Der Grenzbauer*) takes us to the German-Russian boundary line as it existed before 1914; Gottfried Rothacker (*Die Kinder von Kirwang,* 1938) and Josef Ziermair (*Feindschaft auf der Gramai*) extol the fighting spirit of Sudeten farmers. This type of farmer, the *Grenzbauer* or *Wehrbauer,* will of course disappear from the German peasant novel, being as he is an obvious creation of political propaganda and of a twisted conception of history. But it is well to remember that the German peasant novel, much as it has suffered from the glorification of the *Grenzbauer* who is ready to shoot any Pole, Dane, Russian, or Czech for trespassing on German soil, has suffered even more from becoming a scene where anti-Semitism and the open defiance of Christian candour, or of any candour for that matter, are given free rein. The North German peasant novel, with its frequent adoration of German mythological figures, inducing a pagan attitude which almost invariably tosses away all self-control and delights in exhibiting a total lack of concern for other people, or at least for the weaker ones, was to a certain extent corrected, and in some instances attacked and reprimanded, by a more conservative point of view in the South, especially in Catholic Austria. Anti-Semitism, on the other hand, while not openly practised by the South German authors of peasant novels, was at least silently tolerated and thus approved of. Such North Germans as Möller-Crivitz, Paul Seelhoff, and Kurd Schulz, who have every *Erbhof* threatened by a Jewish cattle dealer or real estate agent, seem to have met with no rebuke.[1]

Foreign critics have at times fallen into the error of labelling all modern German peasant novels as products of National Socialism. But farm life has, as often as not, been dealt with by writers of great integrity, and peasant novels will continue to appear. The tradition is firmly entrenched in the literary life of Germany, owing to the inherent qualities of its subject-matter: epic material calling for realistic description, a human psychology which is as rich as and often more varied and more passionate in its reaction to life than that of city-dwellers. Even during the last few years not all peasant novels have been pressed into political service. Many authors have gone on writing of the timeless and typical conflicts which occur on the land no less than in the cities, as when Josef Ziermair (*Der Bruckhof*) treats of a love triangle releasing elemental passions, or when Arthur Rathje (*Weisse und schwarze Erde*) grafts the Enoch Arden theme on a country setting. One or two such peasant novels compare favourably with the best the past has produced.

Erich August Mayer can on more than one count stand comparison with Jeremias Gotthelf. Mayer's novel *Der Knecht* reminds one of Gotthelf's *Uli der Knecht,* first of all because of the

[1]The most insolent exhibition of racial pride and prejudice is to be found in the story of an East Prussian landowner who unknowingly married a Jewess, *Die heilige Nacht der Gonschorras,* by Elsa Wilutzky.

plot: an orphaned boy by dint of hard work, his love of farm life, and an innate fondness for animals becomes all but indispensable to the success of a rich farm, the owner of which, an invalid, has a good-for-nothing son. Secondly, the comparison stands by virtue of Mayer's detailed knowledge of village life which he describes with the greatest clarity, though he holds his naturalistic style subservient to an artistic principle of selection and to a carefully planned composition. To be sure there is in Mayer's novel no equivalent to the profuse leavening of Gotthelf's epics with Christian sermons and Christian ethics. Still, the spiritual atmosphere of the novel is one of moving tolerance and deep understanding. When war breaks out after the shooting at Sarajevo, Friedl, the farmhand, feels first of all that something horrible and dark is approaching. A prisoner of war from Serbia is assigned to the farm, an enemy certainly, but for Friedl a man who had to leave a farm of his own and who now worries, just as he himself would worry, about his loved ones. Friedl is filled with compassion. "War means distress, suffering, despair." "They were children of different nations, but both with the same peasant blood running through their veins . . . they understood one another without exchanging many words." As the demand for soldiers continues, Friedl, hitherto exempted on account of an eye defect, has to join a regiment. After he is erroneously reported dead, the girl destiny had meant him to marry can no longer ward off the advances of a young farmer and she finally consents to marry him, thus walking with open eyes to her doom, a life of toil at the side of a degenerate loafer. Friedl returns at the end of the war, to resume the duties of the simple, faithful worker. His only desire is to save the farm from utter ruin, for the sake of the woman he once loved and whom he still adores.

If Mayer had chosen to end his tale on a note of unswerving loyalty and of love resigned and transformed into devotion and hard work, we should have received a novel both moving and emotionally sound. But for some reason the author decided to dethrone the wicked husband and to reward Friedl's services by a belated marriage with his sweetheart after this man's death.

Mayer summons the *deus ex machina* of the rising tide of National Socialism in Austria, with Friedl being placed on the right side while his rival pays with his life for opposing the march of the victorious Brown Shirts. True enough, Friedl has joined the party because he is genuinely convinced that it will fight for the rights of such poor devils as he. Not exactly a man of great intellectual acumen, he can be forgiven for entertaining such hopes. His rival, on the other hand, is no great asset to any party, least of all to an heroic resistance movement. It is possible that with the lapse of more time the bitter taste of these closing chapters will wear off, either because we shall read them as a mere expedient to solve a knotty problem, or because a kind of amnesty will in due time be declared for the meek-minded and gullible who were taken in by the promises of early National Socialism. For the present we experience the saddening shock that comes to us when the pen begins to spatter at the bottom of a page of superb penmanship.

There are no such obstacles to mar the evenness of *Der junge Daniel*, the story of a farm *élève* by Theodor Heinz Köhler; "The Restless Year," to give the sub-title, issues from both the heart and the mind of a young man who is keenly aware of the ills resulting from the injustices of a system in which one master owns all and exploits all. The author's love for the country does not blind him to the need for social reforms. Köhler is not as maliciously ironical as von Hoerner, whose *Der graue Reiter* ranks as a masterly satire on an all-too-possessive *Hofbauer,* but instead has the gift of observing realistically and of assessing conditions with calm justice and quiet common sense. At a time when German literature seems to have lost much of its former eagerness for critical observation, *Der junge Daniel* evokes memories of a period when the probing of life was the main business of literature. Köhler's intellectual companions—a small group of men, to be sure—are to be sought mainly among contemporary proletarian novelists.

3 Proletarian Life

ONE of the most revealing features of recent German literature is the meagre crop of novels that deal with the life of the lower classes and that are written by men who either have personally experienced the grim reality of proletarian existence or feel compelled by deep sympathy and compassion to describe and discuss it. It is only reasonable to assume that many young German authors come from the humble dwellings of factory workers or farm labourers. What scant biographical information it has been possible to glean, chiefly from an alphabetical list of German writers since 1914 which forms the major and most valuable part of the *Deutsche Literatur der Gegenwart* by Waldemar Oehlke (1942), bears out this assumption. One would therefore expect a strong literary reflection of proletarian reality, either in the form of autobiography, or in the form of realistically employed subject-matter. If we add, as we must, to writers of proletarian origin a number of others who, though from the middle and upper classes, are yet interested in the fate of their less fortunate contemporaries, we should expect to find the proletariat well represented and ably led in contemporary literature. Yet with very few exceptions the recent German novel shows no knowledge of or concern with the peculiar problems, hardships, and struggles that form the lot of the lower classes. Most of the writers who do choose this milieu busy themselves in pushing lower-class characters up the social ladder, or show a sentimental contentment with the precarious life of the proletariat, thus giving the impression that the problems of the working classes, which figured so prominently in the writings of German naturalists, have ceased to exist or at least to be of any great significance. We know that the proletariat in Germany no less

[23]

than elsewhere has been able to better its position only slowly and incompletely at best, and this lack of discussion comes as an ominous sign of something suppressed, or of a betrayal of the proletariat by its own writers who have been bribed away from their milieu to paint a rosy-coloured picture of ubiquitous social welfare and economic peace.

Those few writers who did not yield to temptation relate their experiences of misery and poverty in, characteristically enough, the first person. Obviously their sordid childhood impressions were too strong to be eradicated by propaganda; their first-hand knowledge of deprivation has made them impervious, to the point of defiance, to the official tendency to deny the existence of slums and of an unhappiness that is mainly the result of low wages and social insecurity. They describe what they have seen and felt as victims of adverse economic circumstances, following an almost extinct tradition of intellectual and emotional honesty, making no attempt to show that all is well that ends well, or to insinuate that their own ordeals and those of countless anonymous fellow-sufferers have now become reconciled in the theodicy of a new political harmony. Books of this kind are as if detached from the main body of recent German literature, pursuing as they do their own truth—the unmitigated predicament of poor people in all zones and the incongruity of all help that is not given directly, materially, and abundantly.

Artur Landgraf describes in his novel *Hieselstal* the life, very likely his own, of a student who, having failed in his Ph.D. examination, decides to go out and earn money because his family is in no position to help him any longer. At times it is touch and go whether he will have enough will-power and ambition to attempt a come-back or will become resigned to his new place in life, in the section gang of a railway under construction. For this is not the kind of working student who eats, sleeps, and works with the proletariat and is yet conscious of a strong partition separating him from his associates, which will allow him, in due time, to walk off into freedom. But for the fact that a girl he once loved and then lost to an unscrupulous rival becomes free again to spur his higher aspirations, he might have stayed where he was. Landgraf lived for a time close enough to the real problems of the working man, and he writes about him with understanding and sympathy. However, his contact with the proletarian world being so short, the novel under normal conditions would hardly be classified as proletarian, were it not for the fact that the author remains perfectly unbiased, a warm-hearted observer who makes no attempt to lecture to or propagandize among his fellow-workers. It is this feature which renders the book memorable in a period when so few writers seem to have had the courage or the decency to listen attentively to the proletarian voice instead of drowning it out in waves of high-sounding phrases.

Werner Oellers (*Das beharrliche Leben*) writes of his youth up to the end of his high-school days in a small town on the lower Rhine. His father, a thrifty shoemaker employing a few journeymen, is fairly well off when the story begins, but after the breadwinner has been called up for military service in World War I the family slides back into needy circumstances. It is Oellers' portrayal of this general physiognomy of care that becomes stamped upon middle and lower classes alike, which transforms the book into something akin to a proletarian novel; moreover, his method is admirably fitted especially to take us into the confidence of hard-driven, suffering people, for he observes and records with that combination of emotional warmth and intellectual lucidity which distinguishes the best proletarian novels. While he does not deny that life, even in those lean years, produced some of the everlasting enchantment that is the divine right of youth, he never attempts to sugar-coat the grim realities of want and sorrow; his heart is heavy with the stress of an existence which, instead of being able to unfold its inherent though simple beauty, as it would have done in peace-time, lies bare to the lashings of the war tempest. Oellers' characters bear up bravely, but without pervertedly contending that they like the ordeal. Even if the plight had been worse, as it would have been in a large city with no farms to fall back on for food, one can feel sure that Oellers would have gone on with the same objectivity and with

[25]

the same dislike for the retouching practised by so many authors who, by the time he was writing, had managed so to bribe their war memories that they provided only a glorification of those horrible years.

The real test of Oellers' attitude in the novel comes when, towards the end of the war, some of the high-school teachers return from the army to resume their duties. Other writers have seized such opportunities to wheel in their propaganda loudspeakers, and one becomes apprehensive lest Oellers spoil his record of clear thinking and love for peace. Much to one's relief there is no let-down. True enough, the returned teacher of his novel does not come out with a sweeping diatribe against all wars and their instigators, but neither does he produce the alibi of the Dolchstoss legend; in fact, Oellers makes him avoid all ephemeral political issues in order to concentrate instead on the most urgent pedagogical duty, to guide adolescent boys in their religious and philosophical struggle since the regular instructor in religious knowledge is giving them stones for bread. Even if no dogmatic beliefs are insisted upon, this mentor at least knows how to keep alive among his students a realization of something infinitely greater than man and more majestic than the world surrounding him; in this way the boys will be prevented from becoming narrow rationalists, or, much worse, cynics in a period when despair and disillusionment have tempted so many into casting out all spiritual ambition.

It is not Oellers' fault that more of life and more of its ugly side have not entered into the range of his deeply sensitive observation. However, by a piece of good fortune—good fortune, that is, as far as the tradition of German proletarian novels is concerned—Siegfried Freiberg seems to have emptied the cup of a proletarian childhood to the dregs, an experience which, supported by an adequately realistic style of presentation, has resulted in a novel that we should consider outstanding even if its position were not enhanced by the lack of contenders.[1]

The youth and adolescence of Freiberg—and of Paul, the

[1]*Salz und Brot* (1935). Reprinted in 1944.

hero of his novel—fall in the same period as Oellers', the War of 1914-18. But for Paul there are no guardian angels to soften the impact as there were for Oellers. In fact, the odds are heavily against him long before the storm breaks. The son of an Austrian railway worker, he loses his mother at a very tender age, and spends twelve years with his grandmother, an impoverished woman living in Vienna. After the second marriage of his father to a widow, a mother of two children, our boy-hero is made to join his parents in a middle-sized city. Now fate really moves into position to harass him from all sides. Relations with his step-brothers weave an unending thread of friction and unhappiness through his days and nights; his stepmother is too worn out by adverse economic conditions to be a good mother, let alone a good stepmother. His father tries to make up for his inability to really apply himself to work by periodic stabs at ambitious plans, only to drown the invariably resulting disappointment in drink and in the company of other women. Worst of all, the local high school which Paul manages to attend is a class-ridden institution.

When war breaks out, Paul is thus a youngster with few, if any, illusions; he has already tasted too much bitterness to expect a change for the better from the frenzies of rampant patriotism. His proletarian training, however, proves very handy when it comes to obtaining food from illicit sources and bartering with the peasants of the hinterland. What is more important, he is able to feel, though not to analyse, the common bond that unites all poor people, especially in times of war. He visits Russian and Italian prisoners of war interned outside the city with never a thought of showing them hatred; on the contrary, he thinks nothing of helping these companions in universal misery with whatever services he can render them. Here and on countless similar occasions young Paul acts with a sense of justice and a spirit of humanity that come instinctively, so one is inclined to hope, to a person who has learned to run only one dividing line through mankind, the line that separates exploiters from exploited. Though embittered by the brazenness of those in power, Paul remains cool-headed enough to know that in order to help

their victims he will have to equip himself with more than com-
passionate emotions: courage, knowledge, and good nerves will
be essential if he is to develop into a fighter for freedom. With this
in mind he goes on learning and thinking, though he always
takes time out to join any protest meeting that gathers spontan-
eously among a half-starved population; avoiding the danger of
becoming prematurely doctrinaire, he conserves his energies and
expands his knowledge in order to be prepared for the great
tasks awaiting the men of his convictions. He was a born proletarian leader who might have re-entered German proletarian
literature, on a more active level, had it not been for the cloud-
burst of reaction that was to bury the green hopes of youth—of
authors and their literary characters—under a sheet of hailstones.

Flammen im Emscherbruch, by Josef Michels, takes us into
the industrial and coal mining districts of the Ruhr, which we
see through the eyes of the workers. The realities of a hard life
are all there: miners permanently injured, young boys quitting
school to help support their parents and sisters and brothers, the
low dives where workers leave the pay envelopes which were
meant to buy food for their families. Yet the author softens the
impact of these sordid conditions upon the reader by inserting a
layer of idyllic optimism. He gives a contentment to his principal
characters which stems from their ability to find solace in the
country, or at least in a small garden plot of their own, and most
of all from their belief that time will transform the drabness of
their scene into something more bearable, harmonious. "The
workers will cease fighting with one another and with other
classes . . . their ability to see things in their natural simplicity
will enable them to recognize true values, genuine humanity . . .
the gentle law of love and understanding is bound to prevail,
ultimately . . . the word will make them free. For the word is a
more precious blessing than light. Did not Goethe say so? And
how precious is the light! It is purer even than gold."

Though the story bears out the author's hope for the beneficial
effect of the "gentle law" upon the workers themselves, we feel no
assurance that gentleness will at the same time solve the more

pressing issues between the two classes, the workers and the capitalists; the latter, in fact, are not even mentioned in Michels' novel. He was either too timid to tackle the problem of the proletariat or lacked the bold imagination needed to write of a future in which capitalism would be extinct. He prefers instead to dole out to the workers the small lyrical comfort of an occasional escape into suburban garden plots.

4 Medicine

IT IS natural to find physicians well represented among literary characters in European fiction of the nineteenth and twentieth centuries; their important place in modern society was bound to have its reflection in literature. In recent German writing doctors (including in this term physicians, surgeons, city and country doctors, and others concerned with the problem of healing), farmers, and artists are the three most important layers in an occupational stratification of fiction. While it is regrettable that reference cannot be made to a monograph by Bruno Wachsmuth, on the physician in modern literature,[1] the amount of material available for this survey seems sufficiently large to illustrate, and possibly to interpret, the exalted position of the medicos. The reasons for this phenomenon are, first, the increasing attention paid to health in modern life; second, the search for a deeper understanding of the process of healing; and third, the fact that particular medical problems have become highly controversial topics in which even laymen are taking a great interest.

In approaching the novels of this chapter one might well feel apprehension; this can be allayed at once: no trace of any preparation for, or discussion of, the practice of putting biologically undesirable people to death can be found. In the light of what has happened in Germany we should expect to notice reverberations from this practice in fiction. If we are inclined to feel a kind of relief over the fact that the literary guild did not, in any shape or form, become an accomplice to one of the greatest crimes of our day, this satisfaction quickly diminishes when we ask ourselves whether such silence did not help to condone things which, in normal times, would have been exposed and vigorously condemned by at least a few writers.

[1] *Der Arzt in der Dichtung unserer Zeit* (1939).

The authority of the physician to terminate pregnancy, under certain circumstances, is one of the problems in which medical and social interests meet. Radical writers during the Weimar Republic were free to state their approval of such interference. No evidence of the discussion having been renewed since then has been discovered. Franz Joseph Magg, in an obviously autobiographical account of his life as a country doctor (*Arzt sein*), relates the moving case of a girl who came to him with the blunt request to "help her." But since there was no legal basis on which to render such assistance (the only justification, we are told, would have been some real danger to her life resulting from pregnancy) the doctor turned her out, only to drive her to an illegal practitioner. The death of the girl, after an operation, affects the doctor emotionally, yet it does not produce any remorse for the stern decision he was forced to make. There can be no quarrel with Magg's attitude, which was demanded by the existing medical code; rather he deserves credit for stating the case with all its tragic implications and not embellishing his part in it by assuming the halo of the modern bio-philosopher who encourages unmarried mothers to fulfil their duty to the state and to bear children even if the fathers assume no responsibility. Honest simplicity is perhaps the distinguishing quality of this book, and its very *raison d'être*; if the doctor portrayed in it practises medicine without much religious or metaphysical speculation, he does, on the other hand, interest himself in the social environment in which he works—rural conditions in his case. His realistic, common-sense outlook forms a most welcome contrast to the sentimental, bombastic, or heroic colouring of country life found in so many blood and soil novels. To mention only one instance: Magg's description of the unbearably hard life to which the wives of small farmers remain condemned, with their time for child bearing being incessantly encroached upon by chores and hard seasonal work, stands out as a sober piece of helpful criticism.

The hero of Magg's story is first of all a country doctor, devoted to his duties and claimed by them to an extent that leaves no time for anything except the most incidental participation in the life of the village.[1] The political events of his day flow by without the slightest comment on his part, which seems rather remarkable, for the doctor does, of course, frequent the local inns.

Gertrud Kunzemann in *Wiedergeboren* paints a vastly different picture. The title alludes to the rebirth of a group of characters, with an old doctor in the centre, during the years of the rise of National Socialism. In the end we know that rebirth is to be spelled with a capital R, and is to imply an event affecting the whole nation. If this were merely the story of a few doctors and some nurses who in their spare time discuss politics, distribute handbills, and prevail upon their old chief to come round and join the party, the book would not qualify for mention. Its real interest comes from the character of Renate, an attractive nurse who, just at the time when a young intern falls in love with her, discovers that her father is really only her stepfather, and that from her real father she has received the curse, technically not specified, of being *"erbkrank,"* of having an hereditary disease. Denying herself the right to bear children, and with that the right to marry, she displays a power of resignation which time and subsequent opportunities for romance cannot shake. As this ethical decision has to be supported by an emotional outlet for her strong impulse to love, Renate spends her life in tending the wounded, during the first years of the Second World War, and in aiding a broken-hearted widow whose husband has left her with two children. This most intimate rebirth, the rebirth of refined and yet very practical love, is well motivated and exemplified.

Angela Koldewey, the story of a young woman doctor, by Betina Ewerbeck, first appeared in 1939. An edition prepared for soldiers in 1942 indicates that up to 200,000 copies had been printed by that time. It is difficult to explain the popularity of this novel. An opening scene set in the operating room of a maternity ward, with a young woman in labour, can hardly

[1]For a shocking contrast see Felix Schlagintweit, *Ein verliebtes Leben*; this autobiography of a Munich doctor will interest the student of psychology for the conceit, brutality, and sexual exhibitionism confessed in it.

account for the appeal; nor is the plot of a kind that would compel much interest. The book does give a detailed picture of student life and work, especially the latter, in a medical faculty. Two students, both very devoted to their chosen profession, become good friends and decide to marry one another. Diagnosing herself, the woman learns that a malignant tumour will allow her to live a few more years only. She wants to make the best of her allotted time, first, by giving life to a child (her affliction not being of an hereditary type it is quite in order for her to have one) and secondly, by making herself a subject for research on cancer for the benefit of future patients. She enables her husband to make an important discovery in the treatment of such a tumour as hers. Though the practical application of his work comes too late to save her own life, she draws comfort from the fact that it will help subsequent generations. "Something has been achieved that will be of lasting benefit for the world."

Much depends, of course, on the spirit in which such a sacrifice is made. In this case there is hardly a pathetic word or gesture to mar the impression of an heroic devotion; what these young people are doing they do with a resolute blending of the scientific attitude and sympathy for suffering men. A new type of passion, a professional passion, enthuses these students and young doctors, a fervour no less intense than that which produces heroes on the battlefield or sends explorers into unknown territories, though it is perhaps a much more practical zeal, firmly bounded by reason.

The medical men and women in the works mentioned practise in strict accordance with their scientific training. They have learned their profession from undisputed masters; even if they do not become specialists, they retain something of an academic and exclusive attitude. Conscious of the fact that what they have achieved is the fruit of a long apprenticeship, they become in turn conservative with regard to the tools of their trade.

Yet the process of ministering to suffering people is ever posing new problems and does not permit of fixed boundaries. Psychologists and religious thinkers have their contribution to make to medicine. Quite often progress is furthered by men outside the profession, usually against its opposition and over its heated protests. The impartial onlooker, though fully realizing the danger of quacks, is nevertheless interested in seeing that medical thought is prevented from going sterile and that medicine does not become the concern of a closed profession. If only for that reason, as a reminder of how far an inspired layman may, under favourable circumstances, be able to advance medical methods, *Die andere Maria,* by Hilde Walde, deserves to be pointed out as a work of unusual merit.

Marianne, the daughter of a German apothecary living in northern Italy, becomes the second wife of an Italian country doctor, Guido Hartmann, whom she has long and secretly loved. Much to her dismay, she finds out after her marriage that Guido Hartmann, financially independent and easy-going, makes only sporadic use of his medical training and of the privilege, as she sees it, of being in a position to do something for the sick and poor. The disparity between ethical obligation and lack of a sense of responsibility is the more shocking to her since the country in which they are living, the plains of the Po River, suffers from the scourge of pellagra—a disease called Milano leprosy by the natives, which is caused by a one-sided diet of corn, the staple food especially among the poor. Its symptoms, dark spots showing on the skin, have a strange way of disappearing during the winter, only to return with greater virulence with warm weather, thus producing the additional strain of hope alternating with despair. Within four or five years a person so afflicted will die a painful death, his intestines slowly eaten away by the bacilli. Marianne, once she has become aware of the heartrending misery resulting from pellagra, especially among the lower classes, knows of only one purpose for her life: to help the sufferers. The way in which she now transfers a love unused by her frivolous husband to the poor, and the manner in which this emotional urge to help crystallizes into clarity of thought and the ability to act, are analysed in one of the finest chapters of modern psychological German prose.

With the aid of a brilliant assistant to whom the philandering husband has left his practice, Marianne begins to fight pellagra both medically and socially. She succeeds in her plan to establish a hospital where patients can be looked after and be relieved of their economic fears. Experience soon shows that a rich diet of fruit and juices will retard the progress of the affliction, at least in lighter cases. More than that, some patients who are put on a strict fruit diet show signs of complete recovery. This is as far as Marianne, an outsider in medicine, can go. It remains now for the trained scientist to evolve the abstract principle from her successful treatment and to find ways and means of producing the remedial agent in concentrated form. And who of all people picks up her discovery, to relate it to other observations collected from medical journals? It is Marianne's husband, who at this stage senses that with a little more work a great reputation may perhaps be acquired. Prompted by his vainglorious ambition, and not at all by any reawakening sense of responsibility, Guido seeks and receives all the credit without giving any of it back to his wife. Marianne, however, is a great enough soul not to mind and she can even smile at the queer trick of fate by which this good-for-nothing husband is hailed as a European authority. Life has transformed her into an ethical being. The only thing that matters to her is the result, the conquest of pellagra; personal fortunes are irrelevant.

Marianne has, in short, reached one of the two poles around which a woman's destiny fulfils itself: either to have children and to be a good mother, or to become that "other Mary." At all times some artists have painted the Holy Virgin without her child, Hilde Walde reminds us, thus creating a no less significant symbol. For the highest form of womanhood can exist without reference to a child, its dignity and worth consisting solely in being a loving woman, and in embodying the ideal of universal motherhood. In times of loneliness and despair Marianne reads a compilation of sacred incantations collected from various psalms, mainly to gain strength by experiencing the feeling that the world is one in suffering as well as in hope, and that all men are elements of one God, and of one demon. Her desire to lighten the burden of those who are less fortunate is rooted in religious and social emotions, not in any ulterior longing for fame or reward. Nor does she ever take time out to philosophize about medical problems. If she differs from the ordinary run of medical practitioners, it is because she follows exclusively the promptings of human sympathy, not because she rebels against existing medical science.

In contrast to Marianne there appear, in these German novels, a number of doctors who envisage a closer dependence of medical practice on philosophical thought. They show a more comprehensive as well as a more rational outlook, which enables them to speak of the philosophy of medicine, and in some cases of the metaphysics of medicine. A new prototype of medical doctor is the result.

As often happens, some historical model serves to explain a new conception of man and to quicken our understanding of it. If no German novelist has as yet attempted to conjure up the ghost of old Hippocrates, it is perhaps only because he already has an advocate, Paracelsus, who is invariably referred to as having successfully developed much that Hippocrates was only able to surmise.

Paracelsus as a force in modern German literature, quite apart from his influence on medical writings, presents an interesting problem for literary historians and critics. It must be assumed that his influence will wane from now on, at least until such time as the political motives of his admirers will have been erased from all connotations of his name; the recent Paracelsus revival can therefore be reviewed now with some detachment. German novelists did not take to Paracelsus simply because they wished to rescue a great medical genius from oblivion, or because his colourful life lent itself to epic dramatization. Books of the semi-biographical type, such as Eve Curie's *Madame Curie,* may have encouraged some writers to try the same with Paracelsus, and to navigate a gripping biography through a comparatively little known though highly agitated period of European history. A greater attraction, however, lay in the fact that with Paracelsus there is the possibility of a national theme or myth, and that he allows the Germans to rewrite Goethe's *Faust,* at any rate the titanic Faust of the German commentators, on new terms. This is a classical instance of masked literary imitation, of switching from one national symbol to another without an essential change in meaning. For you can give Paracelsus all the impetuousness and defiance of Faust and at the same time have the satisfaction of plowing a new furrow. Kolbenheyer's Paracelsus trilogy, it will be recalled, was at once raised by the critics to the level of a nationally representative work, and, moreover, in a jargon that was almost bodily lifted from *Faust* criticism.

Pert Peternell, in *Der König der Ärzte,* follows a middle course between competition with *Faust* and the adventurer novel. Written in a trenchant style, a reflection of the writings of Paracelsus on which the author relies to a considerable extent, the story moves much faster than that of Kolbenheyer. The Faustian ingredients are clearly emphasized, but kept under control. To be sure, in theory Paracelsus is here shown to adhere to the supremacy of will over intellect. "God has no will . . . he allows things to happen or prevents them from happening. But willing is the concern of man." However, a good deal of restraint prevents this theory of will from issuing only in restless activity; for if, as Peternell says, the tension between High Heaven and Earth was uppermost in Paracelsus' mind, his life was at the same time consumed with a sincere devotion to society. The novel closes with a statement, which Paracelsus is supposed to have made, that as a medical man he never felt cause for regret, a fact which is less attributable to an inability to admit errors than to a continuously exercised caution; and indeed throughout the book Paracelsus does nothing that would torment a conscientious man with remorse. With all his admiration for Paracelsus, Peternell refuses to put him up on a pedestal as a symbol of German dynamism.

Peternell's moderation, in this respect, is in striking contrast to the attitude of his contemporaries among the essayists, philosophers, and historians of medicine. A treatise by Hans Hartmann[1]

[1]*Paracelsus: Eine deutsche Vision* (1941).

may serve as an example of the humourless idiosyncrasy to preface all of Paracelsus' characteristics with the adjective German, or Nordic, and to make them stand out as superior against a background of French, English, or simply Western modes of thought and action. According to Hartmann not the least of Paracelsus' merits was the insistence with which he recommended German-grown herbs against imported spices. Franz Spunda gives a more sober interpretation of the philosophy of Paracelsus,[1] yet he suffers the fate of other enthusiasts: the imagery Paracelsus uses is so remote from our ways of thinking and speaking, and so different from the diction even of his own day, that no accurate transcription into present-day philosophy or medicine is really possible.

A layman cannot help experiencing a feeling of relief when he comes from the above-mentioned expounders to a book by Werner Leibbrand[2] which purports to deal with the metaphysics of the medical profession. It is to be hoped that this will be among the works which will survive the physical destruction of Germany and that it will become available both inside and outside German-speaking countries. Since this is a very extensive history of the philosophy of medicine, Paracelsus is here relegated to the more modest and for that reason more plausible position of one among many others who had the wisdom to see medicine and the physician as parts within a greater whole, and who endeavoured to define the relationships obtaining between material and spiritual spheres. Leibbrand reminds us that good doctors have at all times tried to base medical knowledge on an intelligent philosophy of nature and to take into consideration the psycho-physical constitution of man. They have regarded illness not as an abstract entity, but as an individually conditioned disturbance. If for the sake of convenience the name of Paracelsus is used to symbolize a more philosophical conception of medicine, this does not mean that the philosophical, psychological, or religious type of doctor has to be a pedantic imitation of Paracelsus.

[1]*Das Weltbild des Paracelsus* (1941). Other recent books on Paracelsus: L. Englert, *Paracelsus* (1941); F. Lejeune, *Paracelsus* (1941); Basilio Telepnef, *Paracelsus: A Genius amidst a Troubled World* (1945).

[2]*Der göttliche Stab des Aeskulap: Eine Metaphysik des Arztes* (1939).

Among attempts to reincarnate Paracelsian medicine in a modern figure that of Kurt Gröbe in *Kassenarzt Dr. Konrad Wege* (1938) seems to have met with general approval. A 1942 reprint indicates that 37,000 copies had been released by that time, an impressive figure in Germany for books of this kind. An array of intimate professional details leaves no doubt that the author is a doctor himself, with sufficient literary talent to turn autobiography into an interesting tale. He, in the guise of Konrad Wege, shows much natural ability for the practice of an integrated medicine, treating as he does not so much academically defined diseases but concrete human beings. "He never treated a broken leg only, or an abscess, or rheumatism, or any other affliction that was brought to him; he always treated the whole human being, whose sufferings are in most cases merely symptoms of a disturbed inner equilibrium." And in his diary he writes: "There is no such thing as an illness, there are only patients." The doctor's work he considers part of a cosmic campaign for peace and happiness. If war is the father of all things, who then is their mother? The answer is: love. But how is the medical man to express such lofty ideals in scientific practice? The heat of emotion has to be turned into the light of reason and of intelligent action. Wege has no answer to this; he practises his medicine of love instinctively, hoping that the future will be able to distil, from intuition and emotion, a rational insight that may develop into new medical methods. He has his own mystic formula to explain what he is doing, although he cannot analyse it in detail: "The physician is the indispensable catalyser for every remedy that is prescribed to bring relief to his patients. If he does not mix himself into the remedy which he prescribes, it will in most cases remain ineffectual." But the individual physician possesses this catalysing power, not of himself, but by an act of grace, which explains why not every physician is in a position to cure every patient.

Wege, however, cannot be called a rebel. He stays, with all his mysticism, inside the sphere circumscribed by the scientific training and information he has received at the university; what goes on outside of it he dismisses as the bungling dilettantism of charlatans. He never stops to consider whether some of the most far-reaching discoveries in medicine were not made in spite of or even against the protests of conservative professionals. For this reason his sympathetic attitude, and the philosophical halo he at times wears, strike one as being embellishments rather than activating forces.

The title of Hans Künkel's novel *Ein Arzt sucht seinen Weg,* "A Doctor in Search of His Path," serves notice of a bolder foray into the medical sphere, and, indeed, here we sense something of the fearlessness and radicalism which, rightly or wrongly, have become associated with the name of Paracelsus. Mart, the hero of the story, is the son of a duly certified doctor established somewhere in the North German heath. Having had to go to war before graduating from the gymnasium, Mart after his return lacks patience to go through a medical course. Instead, he retreats into the heath to take possession of his shepherd grandfather's home. The old man had, in his day, enjoyed a great reputation as an unorthodox doctor, a herbalist, as it were. Taking it for granted that the power of the old fellow has passed into the young man, the people flock to him with all sorts of ailments, and with boundless faith. Mart could, of course, consult his medical books, but why should he? "He yielded to his healing impulse." And he seems to justify the confidence placed in him. "Healing power had accumulated in him and now it was as when the locks in a stream are lifted. Such was the power that surged from him to treat his patients." Two things support him in his practice: he has the gift of discovering whether a patient is destined to recover or to die—he takes on no fatal cases—and he never asks for a specific fee, leaving it to the patient to pay according to his ability and generosity. So Mart settles down, gets married, and becomes widely known and much in demand as a healer.

The author tries to make us believe that the many cures effected by Mart are the result of some mystic power by means of which he is able to release, for each individual patient, his particular vital strength. "Now I know," he confesses, "what until recently I was unable to understand: the cures I have succeeded in bringing about and which struck people as being a kind of miracle, were effected by my ability to turn man's inner urge to live towards the junction where man is joined to the tree of life. I have not performed miracles, but I have given into their hands the root of life." Such metaphors, of course, defy all attempts at a rational interpretation. There is no way of checking these medical accomplishments. If we believe in Mart's cures we must wonder what became of his knowledge, and why we cannot all benefit by it. The question suggests itself: Is the medical man a fit character for a novel? There is of course no reason why novels should be written about farmers, painters, or business men rather than about doctors. But the substance to be developed in medical novels must be taken from human nature, or from medical science and history; it should not be fictitiously scientific or historical, unless the setting is clearly a utopian world. To present a fictitious pioneer doctor who is miles ahead of present-day practitioners, and to write realistically about his methods and the astounding results obtained thereby, will invariably produce, in the reader, the one feeling which the novelist should strive to avoid: the feeling that it is all fiction and not even imaginatively credible. For if such things were true, surely we would have heard about them; our family doctor would have told us. The case is different if such claims are made in novels dealing with doctors who have actually lived and are known to historians of medicine. History will either confirm or dispute their success, and the reader has the assurance of a definite check on the imagination of the author. Hence, we presume, the popularity of the historical doctor, in biographical or semi-biographical books.

The history of German medicine knows of many outstanding characters fit to be revered as medical martyrs or pioneers. Erich Haehl's story of the founder of homoeopathy,[1] Samuel Hahnemann, deserves mention both for the stalwart qualities of this

[1]*Ein Arzt wird Rebell* (1943).

[41]

historical personality and for the literary ability of the author. Typically enough, Haehl introduces his subject as a parallel to Paracelsus, assuring us that much of what the Germans like in Paracelsus—the qualities of a fearless fighter, his philosophical bent, and, no small attraction, the near-tragic fate that was his—may also be found in Hahnemann's life.[1] And Hahnemann could supply a future novelist with even more of the material that makes Paracelsus such an apt subject for fiction: an adventurous life marked by emotional crises, interesting family ramifications, recognition withheld and then profusely bestowed upon him, a second marriage, and a burial plot in the Montmartre cemetery.

We have other evidence that the demand for the medical novel and for the related genres, medical history, biography, and autobiography, is symptomatic of our times. Rudolf Thiel's popular account of German medicine,[2] pegged to a series of immortal names from Paracelsus to Pettenkofer, had had printings totalling 95,000 copies by the end of 1942. Of Rudolf Heinrich Daumann's novel *Patrouille gegen den Tod*, a rather sketchy work dealing with the highly fictitious aerial mission of a group of doctors into the heart of Africa where they gather enough data to produce an epoch-making serum, 60,000 copies were on the market in 1939.

While no definite figures are available for the number of copies produced or sold of Philip Galen's *Fritz Stilling*, the story of a German doctor living at the turn of the last century, it is significant that this reprint of a half-forgotten nineteenth-century novel went, in 1941, into a second printing. It would be easy to argue that the renewed popularity of the book can be explained by an appeal to other than strictly medical interests. The hero undergoes all sorts of privations before coming to the university, and, as a young doctor serving in the Napoleonic wars, at least from 1813 on, he takes us through an exciting historical period. Commensurably with such interesting subject-matter, the author

[1]Another great medical dissenter of the nineteenth century, Jakob Kneip, famous for his cold-water treatments and cures, has found a very able literary portraitist, Eugen Ortner (*Ein Mann kuriert Europa*, 1938).

[2]*Männer gegen Tod und Teufel* (4th edition, 1942).

writes fluently and displays great skill in drawing a variety of characters that can stand comparison with those of a Dickens novel. But when all this is allowed for, the real appeal of the book is that it takes us right into the confidence of the medical profession whose many practical difficulties we follow at close range. Of philosophical pretensions the author has none. Fritz Stilling goes through life without ever having heard of the patron-saint of medicine, Paracelsus. Or if he has, he makes no mention of him. Stilling's own vitality and sense of humour were strong enough to prevent him from idolizing a dubious sixteenth-century figure, at a time when every effort was bent towards the adjustment of medicine to the discoveries made in the field of the natural sciences.

5 Art

NOVELS about artists have always commanded an exalted position in the history of German literature. The author, even when his leading character develops into a painter or sculptor, seems to write of something that is close to his heart and that makes him vibrate sympathetically. Moreover, as a person of great sensibilities, or professionally cultivated sensibilities, the artist personality of a novel quite often possesses a seismographic comprehension of life whose characteristic aspects at any given period he reflects. The reader is also often delightedly caught and carried away by the ability of the hero to probe new levels of existence, even if this ability does not lead to a higher type of life but merely to the expansion or refinement of sensual contacts with reality. Again, the social status of the artist, as it underwent drastic changes in the course of the last two centuries, has provided a problem of considerable fascination.

For the period of this survey, novels dealing with artists have, as far as can be judged, lost their once central position and no longer perform these important functions. If a number of authors still attempt a kind of vitality-transfusion by keeping us in close company with an artist, they do so cautiously, choosing most often for their centre an historical artist personality whose proud sense of individuality can be trusted to have virtually lost the power of becoming contagious.

The majority of artist novels make it their business to show that artists, musicians, writers are as much in need of a rejuvenation through contact with "blood and soil" as is the common man. The details of the plot arise from the fact that the artist takes the medicine only after stubborn refusals, or takes it when every city sophisticate tries to discourage him from doing so and recommends instead useless palliatives. It is some such turning-point in the artist's life, when he sees the light radiating from simple country existence or when his longing for a place of his own among the trees and in the meadows (a little cottage will do) is gratified, that provides the main theme of so many artist novels. Psychological, religious, and metaphysical problems are relegated to a secondary position. The climactic crisis for the philosophy of blood and soil, the sharpest conflict it can produce, is that between life and art. Characteristically enough this conflict breaks out in women artists with even greater violence; fortunately for them, the solution is never in doubt, at least not in the minds of the novelists, who all proclaim that women will invariably prefer motherhood to artistic occupations, whenever the former seems jeopardized by the latter. It is only natural that strictly autobiographical accounts and fictitious biographies of artists should reveal similar tendencies. If to live in close contact with unsophisticated villagers is the consummate fulfilment of an intellectual's life, many of them will themselves move out into the country, temporarily or permanently. And when they have done so and turned rustic, they will of course be eager to inform their contemporaries of their instinctive or even prophetic anticipation of the blood and soil style of living.

It was the good luck of Hans Fallada that he turned part-time or gentleman farmer when such hobbies were not yet considered to be the hall-mark of wisdom and of integration with cosmic forces. When this time came, he held a trump card in his hands and was able to produce a book of an immensely popular appeal—a picture book, the author hastens to explain in the first sentence of his autobiographical tale of a writer's life in the country, *Heute bei uns zu Haus*. Future historians of literature may be tempted to feel that Fallada's book is not really a panegyric upon rustic life and the philosophy of blood and soil, but rather a mild parody of a popular vogue. While nothing would seem more natural than that the official pressure to produce healthy books of the back to the soil type should have induced an exasperated writer to create a modern Don Quixote of the

Erbhof, it is unlikely that Fallada harboured such ironic and courageous thoughts. The scattered patches of humour growing on his farm are the result of Fallada's charming inability to take himself too seriously as a farmer. It is, however, less desirable to find the same inability in relation to his authorship and professional habits, of which the book talks at great length. To hear him discuss the process of creative work, one would think that writing novels is first of all a case of selecting the right kind of paper and keeping the proper width of margin. Not a word is said about the more relevant questions of social and philosophical attitudes. This conception of art as being only one trade among many others, natural as it is to Fallada, whose books have for a long time seemed to be made rather than allowed to grow from the depth of a personality, is at the same time symptomatic of a tendency to minimize the importance of the intellectual, and to apologize for wielding the pen instead of the hay-fork.

Even where a much loftier conception prevails, the primacy of biological life remains undisputed. The problem of art and life is brought to a wonderfully simple crisis and subsequent solution in *Und eines Tages öffnet sich die Tür*, by Walther Kessler. It is hard to decide whether Kessler is merely the editor, as he asserts, of this bulky volume of letters exchanged between a graduate in fine art and a young sculptress or whether his statement is intended to mask his authorship of an epistolary novel. The sub-title speaks of "letters of two lovers," and the 60,000 copies printed indicate that the book was read primarily as a love novel; it might even have been bought as a text-book on how to write love letters. An elevated style, noble sentiments, and the art of wrapping a profuse absorption of every subjective mood in an appropriate quotation might well be learned from the book. The more significant feature of it is that the two lovers, in spite of all the education they have had, will ultimately conform to the blood and soil pattern.

When the young sculptress begins to realize that the possessive nature of her fiancé gets the better of him and makes him try to ride roughshod over her own free development, she escapes to

Paris, there to devote herself to the study of art. She can stand it for a year, but no longer. Taking stock of her prospects she sees only two possible futures: to go home and get married, or to spend more long years of hard work in the studio. The decision comes swiftly and irrevocably. "To do the latter I have neither the power nor the desire. I love you, this is my strength, and my only desire. All I can think of is our life together. And I am deeply filled with a longing to give birth to a child." True, she also mentions that she was obviously not intended to become an independent, artistic personality. But who is to say whether she is right in making such a statement or simply no longer eager to be an independent artist. There is only one solution to her troubles, and it is contained in the last item of the correspondence exchanged between the two, a wire from her fiancé: "Forever yours arriving Sunday 11 30 Le Bourget airfield." The fiancé, characteristically enough, has during her absence in Paris turned to farming.

If the choice is generally for motherhood as against an artist's career, it is not always made with such decisive resolution. Carola Schiel in *Stern und Erde* ties a knot so complicated that she finds it difficult to disentangle it again. The wife of a doctor slips back into her former world of stage lights and make-up; she also takes up again a promiscuous life and runs away with a sailor. After some years she returns, if not to resume her duties as a wife (her place having been taken by the doctor's rustic servant girl) then at least to appear again, after some time, on the stage and to take part in a *Weihespiel* written by the doctor (now dead), a sort of orphic rite celebrated at his funeral. Since there is no reason to transform this artist-woman back into the housewife of earlier days, the change in her can only be entered on her spiritual record-sheet; the old-type actress becomes a priestlike artist, making of her art a sublimated form of motherhood. Obviously Carola Schiel entertained hopes of refining the blood and soil pattern, which in this case would have called for the return of a repentant sinner to her home. She intended to do this by presenting a new conception of art and of the woman artist, a conception in which art and motherhood become one, that is, a spiritual motherhood. It is equally obvious that she failed to make her intention clear, with the result that what was to be an image of the new woman artist remains a nebulous apotheosis of a vague thought.

Marianne Bruns (*Das rechtschaffene Herz*) accepts the doctrine that a woman's place is in the home reluctantly, step by step. The law of nature at first is only strong enough to prevent the heroine, an actress and the wife of a young painter, from turning into a frivolous screen star and running away with an international movie mogul. Mr. Chaladier, temptation personified, elegant, suave, cynical, a dynamo of work and of glib talk, all but succeeds in seducing the woman; a miracle saves her, which she later describes to her husband in these words, using the third person to soften the shock: "An elegant impresario [Chaladier] and a woman were once sitting on the Markus Square in Venice; along came a little girl who had lost her mother and was now crying. Then the woman took the child into her arms and carried it back to the mother. As she returned to the table, Chaladier was in a bad humour, saying that he would never want to have children. But the woman could not forget the sensation of the arms the child had thrown around her neck, and all of a sudden she knew that she wanted to have children. And then she awoke from her trance. She awoke at least partially. She knew that she wanted to have children not by Chaladier, but by another man, by a little painter who sometimes went unshaven and who never dressed stylishly."

The wish for a child does not separate her from her artistic profession, as it did in the case of the sculptress in Paris. It does, however, save her from committing adultery; and when she intimates, soon after her return to her husband, that she will have to ask for leave of absence from the stage because of pregnancy, we feel that she is inwardly prepared to give up her career. Once again the calling of motherhood proves to be stronger than the prospect of fame and a life of ephemeral excitement.

This attraction which the child has for women artists, to the extent of making them gladly resign their careers, has its counter-part in the lure of country life, of a return to the soil, for male artists. The difference is, of course, that the men are not asked to surrender their artistic pursuits, but are merely induced to expose them to the invigorating breeze of the open land. For it is invari-ably, or almost invariably, taken for granted that the renewed contact with the soil will restore that common sense and mental health of which the city is depriving us.

This recurrent pattern of the artist novel shows to good advantage in Otto Gothe's *Sumpferz*. A painter one day appears in a village on a heath; by slow stages he works himself into the confidence of the natives, and when the story ends we see him moving into a house of his own and married to a widow. While no exaggerated claims are made with regard to artistic benefits to be gathered in the country, there can be no question of the great gain accruing to the painter as a human being. He gives up his self-centred isolation, and can soon with his wise counsel, inexhaustible sense of humour, and serious concern for the villagers take on the role of a much sought after mentor; the contacts made thereby and the experience gained will make him an even more contented philosopher about life, a man who is sceptical without becoming cynical, and kind-hearted without turning sentimental. A most intriguing conversion of art into the art of living has taken place, and the record of it is kept in the form of a soberly written but genuinely whimsical chronicle.

The primacy of life over the specialized existence of the artist is, of course, most readily accepted by would-be writers, dilet-tantes, and others who find the going too hard and who are looking for an alibi for their return to less exacting occupations. It is not possible to comment adequately upon artist novels as long as we lack proof of the hero's, or the author's, real experience of the dilemma between art and life. Kurt Ziesel in *Verwandlung der Herzen* tells the story of a group of young people left stranded by the collapse of Germany after 1918. Their leader, a brilliant young violinist, slowly succeeds in making a reality of their vision of a rural settlement, from its beginning on a piece of wasteland.

When the settlement appears to be well under way and to have gathered enough momentum to be left to the care of his associates, he goes on a concert tour. But during his absence a gang of hooligans, labelled, of course, communists, destroy part of it; the artist interrupts his tour and comes back to his friends to build up their collective enterprise anew. It is obvious that the author wants us to consider the decision, and the resignation it involves, an act of heroic sacrifice. But we are unable to take it as such, since we never quite believe that the hero is a real artist.

What exactly are the beneficial forces which the country-side is credited with having and which form the great attraction and miraculous tonic for city-dwellers? At its best, country life is said to draw us together with people doing essential work, tilling the soil, tending the animals, and living a more rounded life. That tilling the soil should meekly be admitted to be more essential than art, writing, teaching, or the carrying on of some business indicates, of course, the absence of a firm intellectual structure to modern life and that the value of the intellect for a properly integrated society is not understood. It is further claimed that living among villagers—and the artist usually does withdraw to a village, not to an isolated farm—places the individual in a definite tradition with rites, beliefs, and rewards in the form of reputation and influence. This refuge of communal traditions, and the lyrical experience of open country—of rushing brooks, roaring forests, and the quietness of the fields—count very heavily with Hermann Stahl (*Die Orgel der Wälder*). Görg Michel, a painter of the Storm and Stress variety who figures in Robert Walter's *Michel Unverloren,* expects from all these influences an enrichment that will enable him to approximate the ideal he has formed within himself: ". . . the ancient masters knew not only how to compose and execute their works, they were, through the medium of their creations, devotees, servants of the Divine. Their simple, traditional conception of God, for them a divine mediator, has, however, long become obsolete for us. Living at the pace we do, we no longer have the leisure needed for contemplation and reverence, but have introduced a substitute for it, beauty, a vague, pale idea. We call it divine, yet the Godhead has to be sought in the growing grass, in the awe and in the delights of one's native soil, in the sorrows and joys of a human eye, or in the butterfly sailing in the sunlight, and in the birth of a star. A child in the lap of his happy mother, without the accessories of a stable, of oxen and donkeys, kings and angels, all this is divine, if we know how to paint as devotees and servants of the Divine." The country-side and the simple functions of life, such as a mother holding her baby, are here invoked to refresh our dried-out religious inspirations.

Michel Unverloren well illustrates the discrepancy between theory and practice, between a high aim prompted by our modern emptiness of substance and the inability to carry it out by sheer will-power. Not that the action of Görg Michel runs counter to the good life (his rejuvenation through contact with the land finally helps to reunite him with the mother of his child, the offspring of his young, irresponsible days in the city), but the texture of the story remains artificial, lacking in spiritual trans-lucence and creative tranquillity.

Other authors, while not setting the goal for their artist characters so high, succeed at least in convincing us of the good result that comes when the artist says good-bye to the city. For Gerhard Lorenz (*Unrast*) the chief gain in a return to simpler forms of life is the circumvention of entanglements in all sorts of irrelevant *bourgeois* problems. He writes of a painter, Kai, who has fallen in love with a city girl, while the woman destined to become his wife looks on helplessly. Not until the upper-class family of the girl interferes with their romance does Kai discover the soothing value of this other woman, a native of the village on the seashore to which they will ultimately retire. It must be said that Lorenz uses no simple black-and-white formula. The city here has an irresistible attraction, and this is valuable, up to a certain point; the girl Kai is in love with has only the one fault of belonging to a conventional family who strenuously object to the marriage of their daughter with a struggling artist. The girl is fond of out-door life and quick to develop an artistic taste; far from distracting Kai from his work she inspires in him a healthier outlook on life.

The value of this city relationship makes it much more difficult for the author to account for Kai's final decision in favour of the country; the crisis separating the two lovers is much more real than in ordinary blood and soil novels. Their separation results from Kai's reluctance to force the girl he loves out of her comfortable milieu, and to expose her to the uncertainties of his artistic career. The girl, on the other hand, is unable to follow him without being forcefully persuaded to do so. When seen in retrospect, this is a thoroughly convincing solution, easier for the girl than for the man because she can return to the *bourgeois* life of her parents and marry the man her father has long ago chosen for her. The solution is harder for Kai, though quite salutary: no more temptation for him to compromise with conventionality; he is thrown back into the struggle for survival and this, we feel, is as it should be if he is to preserve the insistent vitality in his pictures. Marrying the girl from the country and living with her does not miraculously save him, though it does help him to find the appropriate milieu for his creative urges, which from the very beginning tended towards contact with elemental, robust existence.

If anywhere we come close here to the best argument the modern German artist novel can present, namely, that country life helps to free the artist from the fetters of stifling, time-consuming conventions as they prevail among the well-to-do *bourgeoisie*. This is not to say that good people are not to be found in this class, even in large cities—the son of the *Oberregierungsrat* is instrumental in securing for Kai some measure of worldly success. But it does mean that the danger of being drawn into artificiality is greatest within the crowded quarters of the big cities. *Unrast* can therefore be regarded as the best type of blood and soil artist novel, as the one instance in which the doctrine finds, within limits, its proper justification. One has but to compare it with Else Jung's *Die Jensensippe* or with Ell Wendt's *Wir plus drei,* to see to what travesty the back-to-nature cry can lead: all that happens here is the wish for a cottage, and the fulfilment of this wish. There is not the slightest reason to assume that the home in the country will in any way stimulate artistic creativeness.

The return from the city to the farm as to the fountain of youth for tired intellectuals is more often than not the expression of a nostalgic longing that originates in city life. Writers who come from the country and who have had to fight hard to gain a place in the artistic or literary life of the nation can be counted upon to have much more sober feelings about the charms of country life.[1] Maximilian Böttcher's novel *Die Wolfrechts,* while not primarily a discussion of the artist's problem, throws an interesting sidelight on it by turning the blood and soil theory inside out. The writer-hero in this case returns home more by compulsion than by his own free will, and he finds it hard to go on with his creative work amidst all the distractions, to say nothing of the duties, of country life, and in surroundings which with their realistic weight crush all imaginative life. In his difficult task of combining the work of a mill-owner with that of a socially-minded dramatist he turns to Tolstoy for guidance, since the latter had, on his estate, fulfilled the dream of combining and reconciling physical and spiritual interests. "If one could but shape one's life after the fashion of the great Russian! The German Soul too has to be freed from its fetters, Germany must be shown the way to truth and freedom." The last allusion remains obscure, unless it is intended to mean that harmony between physical and spiritual work will by itself lead to truth and freedom. Böttcher, unfortunately, does not elaborate on the problem, hoping perhaps that the name of Tolstoy will speak plainly enough for all who have ears to hear.

There can be no better illustration of the compelling force of the artist-farmer conflict in recent German literature than the fact that even the historical artist novel takes, among other poetic

[1]Hermann Eris Busse with a masterly ironic touch shows both sides of the picture in a short novel *Girlegig.* A farmer becomes a cabaret performer, to return ruefully to the country after some time.

licences, that one by which the regenerative effect of simple life in the country becomes an important factor in the artist's development, as for instance in the life of Martin Schongauer. At a critical stage during his years of maturing the great Colmar painter, in Lina Ritter-Elsass' novel *Martin Schongauer,* slips into the garb of a monk, evades the search of his relatives, and takes service with a farmer. When the farmer dies, he assumes full responsibility for all the work and chores and becomes a well-integrated and respected member of the village community. At the same time his artistic inspiration begins to stir again, as a result, so we are asked to believe, of such normal and natural life. His true identity dawns upon some villagers when they discuss with him their plans to have the local cathedral honoured with a great picture. The hired man, realizing that a singular opportunity is offered to produce the consummate work of his life, declares his willingness to execute the picture under the condition that his anonymity, for all outsiders, be preserved. Though there is no basis for this incident in the life of Schongauer, the episode is convincingly woven into his career, as the preparation for his one towering masterpiece. It is only when the novelist goes one step further and attempts to make us believe that Schongauer's interest in farming was political as well as personal that we begin to suspect the intrusion of propagandistic elements. "No artisan and no scholar should be permitted to live in the city without having first served a year in the country." Schongauer dreams of a German Reich in which the peasant enjoys the same rights as the burghers in the cities and the noblemen in their castles. Of the three wishes which an angel grants him upon his entry into heaven the first one is: "O Lord, give all the farmers in my homeland freedom and the joy of work."

Carl von Pidoll, in a postscript to his biographical novel *Boemo Divino,* about the eighteenth-century musician Josef Mysliweczek-Venatorini, frankly admits that he had scant historical material at his disposal and puts the reader in a position to realize at once that the vast spaces open to the exercise of the poetic imagination were used mainly to advance his personal conception of the ideal artist, as one who combines progressive political interests with musical talent. Now the rallying point for all liberal forces in the eighteenth century, as the author sees it, was the struggle against the Jesuits; he is of the opinion "that the so-called achievements of the French Revolution—liberty, fraternity, equality—in their obvious hollowness and verbosity have little historical weight when compared with the accomplishment of those who defeated Jesuitism. The decisive intellectual or political date of the eighteenth century was not the storming of the Bastille, it was the day of the decree *Dominus ac redemptor noster,* the papal declaration issued on July 21, 1773, which ordered the dissolution of the Jesuit order."

Von Pidoll, unhampered by any obligation to maintain historical accuracy, and well versed in the technique of brilliant storytelling, has of course no difficulty in proving his point, the great danger the Jesuits constituted in public life. From the moment when young Josef Mysliweczek commits the grave sin of escaping from a Jesuit school instead of working off his gratitude for having been accepted as a pupil in spite of his low origin, he runs into his deadliest enemies at every turn of his life. Discovering behind his particular misfortunes the general policies of a sinister world power that chokes all progressive life, he identifies himself with the opposition to the two decrepit branches of the ruling power: the Church and the nobility. Endowed with what the author calls a strange and valuable insight into human concerns, into political as well as moral problems, Josef endears himself to all good-natured and socially-minded people who like him regard the Jesuit obscurantists and a nobility that has become oblivious to its duties as the arch-enemies of noble feeling and clear, scientific thinking. His success as a composer of popular operas never weakens his political alertness and sense of justice, even if the Jesuits do on occasion try to bribe him with promises of being allowed to live his own artistic life.

Von Pidoll—this much we must concede—has created a character which we follow with all our sympathies through the vicissitudes of his life at the eighteenth-century Italian courts. If in the end we cannot unreservedly accept his artistic-political life as an inspiring model to be followed by other artists, this is the result of a kind of paradoxical situation in which the author inadvertently places himself. For if the relatively obscure biography of Boemo Divino gave the author full scope to present his thesis (there is no well-known body of historical facts to caution us to reject the plot or problem, as there is in the case of Schongauer), the hero's relatively unimportant position in the history of music makes us wonder whether we can accept him as proof of the desirability of combining politics with art. It so happens that on a few occasions young Mozart crosses the path of Mysliweczek, and overshadows completely Josef's significance as an artist, no matter how highly we may think of him as a social and political fighter. Our admiration, as far as musical achievements are concerned, switches from the hero of the story to a secondary character in it, to Mozart; we feel that the high value set on a combination of great musical talent with fervent political activities is not verified by history, at least not as it appears in von Pidoll's story. The thesis the author wanted to prove is refuted by the genius of young Mozart who, as far as we are aware, has not the smallest stake in political or social affairs. It goes, of course, without saying that von Pidoll is much too intelligent a writer to insinuate that Il Boemo was, after all, a greater genius than Mozart. That he should wish to extricate Mysliweczek from the neglect into which he has fallen is, on the other hand, fully understandable.

There are a number of other novels centring around well-known artists drawn from the history of music, literature, or the theatre; too frequently their authors aim at little more than a dramatization, which is often, indeed, a mere presentation in dialogue form, of their lives or of certain incidents therein. To see what a more courageous writer can do with his subject we have for comparison two novels on Michelangelo. Heinrich Bauer (*Michelangelo*), bolder than Gerhart Ellert (*Michelangelo*), dwells on two aspects of Michelangelo's life with an insistence that suggests a strong undercurrent of some special interest. There is, first, Michelangelo's great admiration for Savonarola, whose violent death he bewails with immense grief, and, second, the rugged independence with which Michelangelo protects his integrity as an artist, even at the risk of antagonizing some local tyrant. He, for instance, refuses to assist in the erection of fortified places by which despotic Alexander hopes to keep the city of Florence under his thumb. Taking a stroll one day to the place where construction of one of the fortresses is under way, he is seized with indignation. A farmer happens to come along, and a poignant conversation takes place between the two. That it is the farmer rather than the famous painter who airs his oppressed feelings makes the accusation seem all the more general, coming as it does from a simple, common man. Of Michelangelo's attitude in such matters we are informed in a more indirect way. "Michelangelo seized the old man by his wrist: 'How long is the fortress going to stand? My hair is grey, yours is white, shall we live to see it?' 'Tyrants and walls,' the old farmer replied, 'fall faster than leaves from the tree, sir, once the time has arrived. Don't you see that the leaves are turning yellow and the faces of the tyrants pale? They make a mighty splash for a while, but then earth and plough drive over their skulls, the walls crumble, and in the spring the blades of grass wave in the wind.' " Michelangelo's life is here depicted as one continuous effort to remain free in every city he works in, and to shake off all encroachments upon his physical and moral independence. Ellert, on the other hand, turns the same biographical material into a gripping yet pointless tale of intrigues and of incessant quarrels among the great artists of the period.

Transplantation of historical characters into a novel has its difficulties. Where the personality in question happens to be a well-known literary figure such difficulties seem to multiply, since more attention will have to be paid to written, authentic records left by the hero; these often cover large parts of his life and narrow the space available for imaginative changes or additions. Thus any parts of a novel dealing with the intellectual life of a writer are bound to be a transcript, if not a verbatim repetition, of his letters, diaries, and other such documents. In other instances the historical background has to be reconstructed in detail, in order to attract attention. There remains, in a few cases, the telling of an interesting life-story, or of some emotionally heightened episodes.

Franz Grillparzer would seem to be poor material for a novel, not because of any lack of intrinsic interest in his inner or outer experiences, but because he has left a fairly complete record of them in his diaries and autobiographical writings. Any gaps that he left have long since been filled by his biographers. Friedrich Schreyvogel's novel *Grillparzer* has no higher ambition than to present a biography padded with much superficial but entertaining material—an all too comfortable enticement for students to bypass the sources.

What draws a novelist into the vicinity of Frederick Hardenberg is fairly clear—his romantic infatuation with Sophie, an episode that produced two equally captivating phenomena, captivating at least for people with mystic propensities, namely a release of poetic and philosophical utterances in Novalis, and later (when his fiancée fell victim to an unknown illness) a strange healing faculty which Novalis discovered in himself. Unfortunately there are limits to the use which can be made of this power as literary material, since the relief Novalis provided was only temporary. As to the new spiritual world opening up before the eyes of the poet under the inspiration of his love, here, too, little scope is given to the novelist; Novalis' collection of aphorisms and his letters contain more material than the expert novelist will care to use. For further source-material there is the authentic incident of a visit of Goethe at Sophie's bedside, a series of idyllic views of the Thuringian country-side, contact with pietist circles, and also, by way of contrast, a coarse-grained father-in-law who would be as popular a contributor to a modern stag party as he was in his own day. Less convenient for a novelist who wants to make much of the spiritual forces lifting the love between Sophie and Novalis into mystic spheres, is the undeniable fact that the poet, soon after the death of his one and only love, became engaged to the daughter of a French *emigré*. While Robert Janecke (*Friedrich und Sophie*) closes his account before he has to confess the worldly relapse of his mystic hero, Maria Schneider (*Dichter, Tod und Liebe*) is not afraid of discussing it fully, hoping probably that the death of Novalis, before he had time to consummate his marriage, will be remembered as the answer to the last and irresistible call of Sophie to join her.

In normal times the material offered by the Novalis-Sophie constellation would hardly attract much attention, unless it were supplemented by a mystical-philosophical imagination such as that of Johannes Schlaf who many years ago (1906) presented Novalis as the prototype of a new mystic eroticism. Neither of the two recent authors adds much to what the factual sources will yield; they follow the path of their principal characters with a sober realism tempered by an obvious affection for its strange, mysterious implications, knowing and expecting, so we surmise, that this dry presentation will suffice to remind their countrymen of the existence of an inner world and of its possibilities, and to constitute a protest against modern exhausted sensibilities that can no longer respond to the spiritual and immaterial. Mild as such a protest must appear, it is at the same time irrefutably effective, since the world into which Novalis takes us did exist, and may be brought into existence again as a refuge for those who find our present conception of reality stupidly narrow. Instead of trying to win popularity by showing that the artist is just as ordinary a being as everybody else, and happiest when he can return to simple life, Janecke presents the poet as one who will lead us into new lands. It is significant that yet another author, Fritz Meichner (*Landschaft Gottes*, 1937), attempts much the same thing, again taking the precaution of hiding himself behind an historical personality, the romantic painter Caspar David Friedrich, whose actual experience of blissful piety cannot be easily refuted.

Students of Novalis have long known that his mystic propensities were balanced by a realistic attitude to social and professional matters. Both Janecke and Maria Schneider eagerly seize upon this point and endeavour to have their ethereal poet accredited as a man of the world. Obviously in order to show that mystic inclinations are not in every case tantamount to escapism but may well combine with a practical outlook on life, both novels represent the Christian artist as well qualified to help in the solution of political and economic problems.

No such concessions are made by Emil Barth in his reincarnation of the Sappho myth (*Das Lorbeerufer*), in the form of a young woman growing up on the shores of the Mediterranean Sea. The scene is of a timeless, classical kind; the young poetess has pledged herself to forgo the natural calling of a woman, provided the gods will grant her the gift of expressing her experience of a bitter-sweet world in poetry. But a time comes when she wavers. In the sulphur mines of her uncle she has met a young slave whom she rescues from the hands of his exploiter. The story follows the classical pattern even in its names. The poetess Diana is soon to lose her Phaon to a less austere country girl; the sweetness of love turns for her into bitter sorrow from which she, too, just like her ancient model Sappho, can find release only in her songs. In the ecstasy of forfeiting the sensual world and recapturing a spiritual existence Diana decides to die. There is, of course, nothing original about this plot unless it be the almost irritating nonchalance with which the author trails the ancient myth. It is here that we sense the deliberate intention of going counter to the popular theme and of proclaiming anew the other-worldliness of great artistic creators. The coolly executed marble statue of this *poetessa* begins to assume life when we experience it as an aristocratic attitude for which the world is but the raw material for a perfectly wrought stanza.

The lives of great actors usually make interesting reading without much retouching. When the facts are that the idol of a whole city, as Alexander Girardi was for Vienna, started out as a plumber's apprentice, and became the friend of an emperor and the object of hatred among his enemies who all but succeeded in preferring a charge of insanity against him, no great imaginative exertion is required to round off a good story. Anton Maria

Girardi, the grandson of the actor, has no other ambition than to illustrate a small segment of cultural history in *Das Schicksal setzt den Hobel an*. Time is likely to enhance the charm of this documentary novel, now that so much of its material background has been lost beyond retrieving. By a happy coincidence the milieu in which Girardi reached the zenith of his fame has found another literary embodiment in which it is preserved for posterity, this time by a qualified historian of literature, Heinz Kindermann.[1] His interest is in the organic integration of Raimund's work with the Austrian tradition, whereas Girardi is satisfied to work out the stranger than fiction features in the life of his grandfather.

Johannes Günther in *Sturz der Maske* missed a good chance to construct an interesting novel around the mentor of German actors, Konrad Ekhof, chiefly by neglecting to make full use of a formative phase in the history of German theatres. Instead, the author obscures his hero in a cloud of semi-philosophical commentaries on the exalted position which the art of acting is supposed to hold in civilization. Ekhof's young rival, Friedrich Ludwig Schröder, was much more fortunate in having his eventful life recorded by an author, Hilde Knobloch (*Der Feuergeist*), who puts the weight where it belongs, that is on the historical material.

[1]*Ferdinand Raimund* (1940).

6 *Education*

GERMANY has seldom offered that compact continuity of social life out of which a series of *romanciers,* in the French sense of the word, could have arisen to depict, criticize, and refine national and individual *mores,* but it is nevertheless true that out of German cultural life has, from time to time, crystallized a vision of what ought to be, or an inspiring account of how some gifted being has absorbed the cultural environment, for his or her enrichment. Obviously the educational novel, if it is to be more than a recollection of school-days, requires in its author an individuality of great perspective bounded by self-discipline. Freedom of thought, even intellectual boldness, is essential in the exploration of a region of existence where man's highest intentions can be realized.

Where such freedom of thought is lacking, the educational vision is bound to narrow; men, instead of defining what ought to be, will be satisfied to recommend what is, or even to support what ought not to be. That the educational novel did not suffer more than it actually has suffered from the imposition of state-controlled "ideals" comes as a surprise. For quite a few writers have dared to do their own thinking and to pursue an independent educational path.

The typical pattern of the educational novel officially sanctioned during the reign of National Socialism is as simple as it is provokingly barren. The hero, whose life is supposed to exhibit representative and inspirational qualities, is invariably a young man who, after the defeat of Germany in 1918, sooner or later refuses all co-operation with the Weimar Republic. Instead, he either goes underground to wait for the call to national rebirth or brazenly defies all the laws, customs, and expectations of a

[62]

struggling democratic order. By his actions he will lose many of his former World War comrades or antagonize his own family, and this gives him a semblance of independence and of that false heroism which has done so much to raise naïve puerility to the status of moral courage.

Das innere Bild, by Annaliese Spriegel, is typical of these irritating simplifications that appeared in Germany after 1918. The title refers, of course, to the inner vision guiding a returned soldier, Rainer Randt, through the political and moral dangers of the Republic. His middle-class family connexions, and the devilish schemes of Jewish business friends all but down his spirit. Ultimately, however, the memory of his heroic captain in the army and the rabidly nationalistic attitude of his wife bring him to his senses and induce him to join the National Socialists. A bullet fired from ambush by a political opponent puts a premature end to his activities, if it is not also a punishment for his all too long delayed conversion.

Ulrich Sander, in *Axel Horn* (1938), probably was the originator of the official pattern. After his return to civilian life, Axel, fed up with war and politics, falls out with his friends, who refuse to acknowledge defeat: "The battle," so one of them says, "has been changed into political meetings, the bullet into a newspaper, the grenade into thought." Axel marries and settles down, though not for long. He tires of his wife and feels a growing affection for a paragon of Nordic beauty; proportionately he discovers the fine qualities of the "National Reformers," whom he finally joins. But the hero pays for his convictions, or for his prolonged luke-warm attitude to political interests, with his death by a traitor's gun. If the reader feels any regret over the death of Axel Horn, it is a sort of retroactive regret. In his earlier years Axel was as promising a young fellow as ever went through a German gymnasium, physically proud and intellectually keen, the prototype of the young man who will draw inspiration from only the purest sources in thought and art, a leading personality in "perhaps the first generation of matriculants who after passing their examination did not get drunk." His disinclination, after

[63]

his return from the battle-field, to take part in the activities of subversive, anti-democratic organizations comes much more naturally than his subsequent participation. It is an almost shocking case of a fine literary character trying to go his own way but forced off his predestined path by the author, whose talent at this juncture yields to the powers that be.

Kurt Eggers' voluminous *Tanz aus der Reihe* is clearly an autobiographical work. The hero of the story bears the name of the author, and (a much more convincing proof) his attitudes and experiences are of a kind that can only be lived, not imagined. Too young to have fought in the First World War, Eggers makes up for lost opportunities to become a hero by every possible manifestation of infantile exhibitionism. As a teen-age boy he goes out of his way to antagonize a war-weary, famished population by sporting a uniform and preaching a struggle to the finish when the front is already crumbling. The boy's hatred then turns against those whom he holds responsible for the Armistice and the Treaty of Versailles: Erzberger, Rathenau, Ebert, and the Jews and socialists in general. He is, of course, still at the gymnasium, a pest to his teachers but an object of admiration to the gentile section of his class-mates, if we are to believe the author. His good reputation, so he claims, comes from his readiness to use his fists on Jewish boys, and his instigation of a boycott against the Quakers who had come to feed needy children. "There was considerable excitement in the school when I declared that I did not care to receive help and accept gifts from the Americans whom no one had forced to wage war on us and to hasten our defeat." In fairness to his teachers it must be said that they have nothing but contempt for this boy, and that they feel greatly relieved when all of a sudden he leaves school to join a *Freikorps* on the Silesian expedition. The minister of his parish, on the other hand, shows greater sympathy for this misfit when the question of his being confirmed is discussed. "I pointed to my Swastika. 'How does that harmonize with the Bible, my dear parson.' He patted me heavily on my shoulder: 'I can't stand the Jews either. After all, I am a Protestant minister, and not a Jewish rabbi.' "

Eggers' description of the Silesian intermezzo with the *Freikorps* is a pathetic piece of would-be hero psychology. His participation in a few insignificant brushes with a group of adventurers on the other side of the line is described in the language of world war strategy; the boys roll up the front and execute Cannae pincer movements. By the time he goes back to Berlin his boasts have acquired definiteness and become reminiscences of actual deeds and events. Having been expelled from school during his absence, he is, strange to say, only too glad to be accepted as an apprentice by a Jewish business firm. His forwardness brings about his dismissal, and he next goes to a farm. The abortive Kapp Putsch quenches all hopes for military glory, and he decides to work hard towards his matriculation. It is then, when he has acquired the right to attend university, that life lives up to its reputation of being stranger than fiction. Of all things, Eggers chooses to take the course in theology. However, on second thought this decision appears less strange. Street hooligans do not usually try to interfere with some bawdy party going on in a low dive, but instead prefer to disturb a meeting of the Salvation Army; Eggers must have sensed that he stood a better chance of getting on the nerves of his fellow theology students, than on those, let us say, of students in an engineering school. His life is shaped by the subconscious desire to antagonize people with as little real effort or danger to himself as possible.

The intention to hurt designs its fitting mask, as always in such cases. Eggers conceives of a new German theology which is to take the place of the Jewish-Mediterranean variety of Christianity. "To Hutten I felt attracted, while Luther was unable to move my soul.[1] But Melanchthon I really hated, I did not like this example of the super-intellectual, scholarly, lifeless theologian. Thomas Münzer made a far better impression on me." A visiting professor of theology, Tillich of Leipzig University, helps him, by way of antithesis, to clarify his own Christian concepts. "He spoke of the coming reign of the Lord before which nations and races would disintegrate; the men and women sitting at his feet

[1]Eggers is the author of two novels about Hutten: *Hutten* (1934), and *Der junge Hutten* (1938).

[65]

thought they were exceptionally good Christians because they were listening so intently. They did not realize what kind of masters they were serving, inexperienced as they were. For the audience consisted of republicans and of Jewish and communistic students, in addition to all those townspeople who felt loyal to the spirit of Geneva.[1] The following day I met a theology student, who in my presence dared to speak highly of Tillich and who, with a glance towards me, ventured to claim that every truly human being must feel that he agrees with Tillich. I told him that I should like to box his ears. Because the young fellow only smiled sarcastically, saying that such apparently are the arguments used by the nationalists, I hit him, to be sure with very little force, as he was physically my inferior. With equal sarcasm I asked him to turn his other cheek as well. But he preferred to report me to the president of the University."

Disgusting as the scene is, there are others to surpass it. As a partial fulfilment of examination requirements Eggers has to give a sermon in the university chapel. He turns the event into an occasion for a burlesque show, with his fraternity friends occupying the front rows. Despite all this, Eggers in due time is ordained and even given a position out in the country. It is only when he overreaches himself in propagandizing National Socialism from the pulpit that his superiors ask for his resignation. Fate has caught up with a ruffian who mistakes himself for a rebel. For in spite of the invocation of Nietzsche, here and there, Eggers' philosophy remains a concoction of high-sounding phrases drawn from an arsenal of demagogical promises, and the compelling power behind his actions is a thinly disguised attempt to acquire by stealth such power and influence as come to serious and hard workers only, at least in normal times.

What makes Eggers' story so revolting is our feeling that he means exactly what he says and that he undoubtedly committed all the acts of rudeness his hero boasts of; perversion had corroded the author's mind long before it corroded his literary characters; we bow our heads in shame while reading his book. It is hard

[1]The latter reference is presumably to the League of Nations.

to conceive of a more disgusting report on German youth than the one this book contains. Historians interested in the psychological veins that ran through the German nation after 1918, will welcome Eggers' book as source-material, not because it unravels great mysteries of human nature, but because it confirms what decent people are apt to forget: that some men are born braggarts and become brutal by a strong natural inclination. If a character like Eggers' occurred in more than one place in Germany, if a book like his was able to strike a sympathetic chord in more than a handful of German youths, then we are a step closer to the explanation of the excesses perpetrated during the National Socialist régime. The reading of this nauseating novel helps us to understand that a few men are sufficient to corrupt a whole nation, a good nation no less than a weak one.

Perusing Veit Bürkle's account in *Lasst das Frühjahr kommen* of how a simple villager, Godson, comes out of his isolationist shell after the last war to join the Party and to take a lead in cleansing the local district of all republicans, we cannot help experiencing a measure of hilarity. Obviously the author tried hard to outdo the regular pattern of the official educational novel in the illustration of miracles performed by converts to National Socialism. But he overstrains himself and the events he describes assume a wholly fantastic character; having no selective power over his imagination, and no store of personal experiences to work with, Bürkle is unable to control his train of conjured-up fantasies. Godson, among other exploits, wins the love of a beautiful widow, the daughter of a retired colonel; they are married and in due time a child is born to them. Unfortunately nature has forgotten to provide the mother with a constitution which will enable her to nurse the baby. But the spirit of comradeship, as it develops among members of and sympathizers with the Party, comes to her aid. In steps a former servant girl of the Godsons. When she had first seen the woman Godson was to marry (the girl herself secretly adored him) she had had her misgivings about the future Mrs. Godson's ability to feed a son and heir; so, in order to be able to give assistance, she had managed to become pregnant herself, and to have her illegitimate child at about the same time that Godson's child (a boy, of course) was born.

Better writers than Eggers had their misgivings about the general trend of things during the Weimar Republic. Whatever conclusions they arrived at, whatever the remedies they recommended, none of them advocated the crudely demagogic methods of Eggers. It will be interesting to see, when all the literary material of the Hitler period becomes available, what course other principal characters pursued in German fiction during the twenties and thirties. It is significant that some novelists of more than ordinary merit betray no knowledge whatsoever of the panacea for all ills offered by the National Socialists. True enough, most of these novels with that blind spot for the blessings of the *Führer* are of an unrealistic type. A few novelists, however, start with a firm conception of the actualities of the period and surprise and please us therefore all the more with their unwillingness to lead the hero, after he has been duly educated and tested by destiny, into the fold of the Party. It might be well to take note of such authors, who, though acknowledging the existence of National Socialism, refused to surrender their independence of thought and living. In doing what they did they must have known that they became open to grave suspicion.

Of novelists who seem to have kept their mental reservations against the régime, and to have been able to express them by devious artistic means, two deserve special mention: Ottfried Graf Finckenstein, and Albert Lorenz. The former produced a remarkable story of a cultured and intelligent young German holding out, as long as possible, against National Socialism. To be sure, it is easy enough to point out that the hero of *Dämmerung* does finally sign on the dotted line of a party membership card; but he would have to be a very naïve reader indeed who would take this step at its face value, for not only does the story, and the life of the hero, fade out immediately after the conversion as if in protest against it, but what is more, while undergoing the process of political re-education at the hands of a party stalwart, Eduard von Reiherberg, the obstinate disciple, loses no opportunity to defend his recalcitrance and to poke fun at the mob psychology which he is invited to share. If in the hour of his surrender he forgets all the brilliant objections he had raised before, the reader surely will never forget them—and that might well have been the deeper intention of the author. In their entirety these objections form the best refutation of totalitarian tendencies one could think of. An aristocratic background, his cultural inheritance, natural intelligence, and an acquired knowledge of other nations, especially the United States, enable Eduard to conceive and to express all the aversion a self-respecting man must feel for a political philosophy of soulless *Gleichschaltung* that (to use his own expression) reduces its adherents to an ant-like existence. He does not mince words about his opinions, rather, he goes out of his way to be blunt when deflating the phraseology of his would-be saviour, a bullying party boss. Eduard professes deep suspicion of all world conquerors, because, as he says, they will always bring more misery than good to mankind; he feels, and states, that the practice of dynamic living is whipping the last resources out of the nation, a process which cannot go on forever.

Yet in spite of many satirical stabs we cannot, with certainty, claim that Graf Finckenstein is satirizing, with his tongue in his cheek, the pattern of the official educational novel, the conversion of a reluctant young man to National Socialism. The case may well be more complex, and involve not only ironic criticism but also final acceptance to avoid further annoyance. Tired of an overstrained individualism Eduard makes his peace with collectivism, with a collectivism he really disdains. The author, rather than allow his much-tormented hero to lapse into the ironic mood which is bound to reclaim him, prescribes a quick death on the battle-field and thus ends the vexing emotional dilemma.

Unter Gottes Gewittern, by Albert Lorenz, is as perplexing a book as *Dämmerung,* though for very different reasons. While the latter is spiced with such irony as is not easily found in German literature of this period, the former is serious to a fault. Young Pastor Wietfeld, the central figure of the novel, has in his inexperience married a conventional middle-class girl. Upon meeting a beautiful actress he realizes his mistake and wakes up to the possibilities of a richer physical and intellectual life. At the same time his theological beliefs pass through a deep crisis, which leaves him with a burning desire to establish a more immediate contact with the Godhead than his church provides. It is not, as with Eggers, a case of politics usurping the place of religion; Wietfeld dreams of a revitalized Christianity willing to cope with social problems. "I want to see Christianity and piety renewed in our nation, to form a strength-imparting belief, which the nation will need in the great world struggle that is approaching. If it is not possessed of a true belief in itself and in God, the nation will break down." Every man is, or ought to be, a Christlike being. When, in his search for a more inspiring Christianity, Wietfeld encounters National Socialism he does not throw in his lot with the movement; he has already penetrated to a depth of thought that forbids him to compromise with anything less sincere and inspired than his own vision. Not finding a group that he can join without becoming untrue to his ideals, he is driven into isolation; finally he takes on the role of the one and only true prophet and leader, as if he had never heard of Germany being blessed with the gift of the *Führer*. Thus at a mass meeting which he happens to attend, fired by the conviction of possessing the real message for the nation, he usurps the part of the main speaker and delivers a soul-stirring speech. Hardly has he finished when all of a sudden there is a flash of lightning, followed by thunder, and the prophet lies dead on the platform—a strangely fantastic scene in an otherwise realistic sequence of events.

While the author, to dispel official misgivings, could always explain the thunderbolt as a swift punishment of *hubris,* it would seem more appropriate to read a symbolic meaning into the event: there being no chance, under National Socialism, for a saviour to succeed, Providence removes him from the scene, probably to preserve him for a more opportune time. This piece of psychological symbolism comes naturally, though boldly and unexpectedly; by it the author reveals the burning ambition of his heart, to deliver the nation single-handed from decadence, from its lack of true religion and its surrender to materialism, a task which he can entrust to no one else—not even to Hitler. We cannot help sympathizing with him; even if his conception of a new Christian way of life lacks humility, it contains at least the hope of a continuing tradition of humaneness and respect for the lives of others.

The principal character in *Gestaute Flut*, by Walter Kramer, is as good a boy as can be found among the youth of any nation. Though of humble origin, Gerhard Haltendorf manages to absorb life in all its richness, first as a youngster growing up in the Saale valley with its stores of natural beauty, folk-lore, and interesting human contacts, then at the Eisenach gymnasium, and later in Berlin as an engineering student. A strong temptation to develop an unusually promising talent is mercilessly suppressed once Gerhard realizes that he has not really the voice to become a truly outstanding singer. The shots of Sarajevo put an end to these years of steady growth, as they do in so many other novels of the same period. Returning from the war with an enviable record of quiet heroism, sacrificial devotion, and duty fulfilled, though without tangible rewards, he goes back to his native town, to find that conditions there are hopelessly out of joint. The moral disintegration, as the author sees it, is proceeding in two directions: the old and honest, though inert, leaders in the community have been replaced by a clique of big-mouthed, vulgar upstarts whose only concern is to make hay while the sun shines, and to eat, drink, and be merry. At the same time there have sprung up in remote and romantic parts of the country-side strange sects preaching the gospel of complete abandon to nature; they let their own hair grow and they allow everyone else to indulge his or her own whims. To use one's will-power is anathema to them. Gerhard remains firm in his conviction that the future must be rebuilt with the best counsel the past can offer, though radical changes and bold readjustments may have to be made. A synthesis of tradition and revolution, of nature and intellect—this is the goal he sets himself. "Be yourself but do not remain yourself"; "God is greater than nature."

Kramer must, at this juncture, have been conscious of the

[71]

opportunity to show that a man of Gerhard's fine qualities was just the kind of youth to wear a brown shirt and to enhance the reputation of the Party. He bravely resists the popular solution though he does not openly challenge the demagogic siren calls. What he does with his hero can be best described as an escape into symbolism. True enough, the building of a power dam in the vicinity of his native town, which from now on forms the point of reference for Gerhard's life, would ordinarily be accepted as a realistic event. Yet in spite of all the details of geology and engineering we cannot read this last part of the book with the same sense of chronicled reality which the first part gives. We know too well what went on in Germany at the time of this supposed construction of a Saale dam. Gerhard has not a word to say about the political struggle that shook his native country, a silence which is all the more surprising as it contrasts strangely with his former interest in and running comment on the affairs of the nation. We regret this withdrawal from reality into symbolism by which a strong and righteous character is lost to social life.

For compensation we have the intended meaning of the symbol. The dam speaks, first of all for itself, as a piece of communal action undertaken at a time when most people were either talking or listening to talkers. Furthermore, since the dam will submerge the old town and necessitate its being rebuilt on a new site, the author is provided with a means of illustrating what, in his opinion, should be preserved and what deserves to be scuttled for good. Two institutions must be saved and rebuilt on an even better foundation: the school and the church. The emphasis put on the forces these two institutions stand for brings out once more the *leit-motif* of Gerhard's educational philosophy. Schooling is essential even if there is a danger of its becoming a study of merely formal knowledge, of purely intellectual abstractions; religion will always have its irreplaceable function, to serve as a reminder of the greater mystery enshrined in the mystery of worldly existence and as an admonition to us to acknowledge, in all modesty, a mind greater than ours. If man,

[72]

in his Faustian urge to penetrate into the secrets of life, should come to realize that the essence of all being is love, then he will have reached the limit of the range of worth-while knowledge; there will remain for him, from then on, nothing to do but to enact the spirit of love in his own immediate environment.

The reminiscences of Faust seem natural in this connexion. Kramer's hero shares with Faust the belief that the untiring effort of man will of itself recognize and achieve its final goal. In the definition of this goal Kramer is, however, much more explicit than Goethe, perhaps because he was well aware that there were enough advocates among his contemporaries of dynamic energism but few voices to caution against the unbridled release of will-power. Our urge to do things must be guided by our responsibility for the well-being of society.

It is gratifying to discover that yet another mature educational novel, *Die Jünglinge,* by Willy Kramp, leads up to an equally outspoken condemnation of the unadulterated will to live and will to power. The fact that in this instance the gospel of everybody for himself and the devil take the hindmost is preached by an itinerant American philosopher will deceive no one. What the author intends is the castigation not of a foreign but of a home-grown titanism, of a tempter promising all the riches of the world if one is but willing to cast aside all moral scruples and all restraint. Dr. Sneeders, the American prophet of a fashionable egotism, speaks the language of German irrationalism and voluntarism. "Dear friend," he says to a youth arguing with him, "why do you revolt against your own power? Let me tell you: a man with power is free to do what he wants to do, he may even do what other people call evil, for such evil will become sanctioned by the very excess of power that compels him to commit evil deeds. There exists only one kind of innocence in the world, the innocence of power." The influence of Nietzsche, in this and other passages, is obvious. Young Count Gortz, the leading character in the novel, is however in no danger of succumbing to the philosophy of untrammelled power, though Eva, his sweetheart, does find it attractive and runs away with the apostle of ruthless self-expression to be his secretary and to become his mistress, only to find herself after some years a broken soul and a wasted body.

The encounter with the great temptation of power is not the only test to which Kramp's young men and women must submit, though it is the most decisive one. Gortz, his step-brother, and a friend of theirs, the son of the pastor in their native village, could perhaps have gone through life without taking the trouble to worry about and experiment with new forms of existence. The semi-feudal background in East Prussia from which they spring would have provided them with a comfortable berth. But the experience of the war has shaken their confidence in the traditional ways of life and aroused their intellectual curiosity and their sense of moral responsibility. So they all leave the countryside and proceed to Berlin, the pastor's son to study theology, Gortz's step-brother to study medicine, and Gortz to prepare himself for the duties of a great landowner by taking courses in economics. Interested as they are in their chosen subjects, they consider their university years mainly an opportunity to find a philosophy of life and to get their bearings in a swiftly changing world. Once more it is the turbulent time of the Weimar Republic into which the author pushes his searching characters. Again, as in Kramer's *Gestaute Flut,* references to actual events as the historian knows them are few, if any; instead, we get what the author may have thought to be the essential features of the struggle.

One of the questions these young men have to answer concerns the demarcation of the sphere they may hope to influence. Should they think of the nation as a whole, of the Reich, or should they restrict themselves to the more concrete reality of the immediate environment? The decision is two to one, against the far too abstract concept of the nation. The dissenting vote comes from the theology student, who runs around organizing action groups that aspire to control public opinion and to raise the level of collective ethics by holding meetings, distributing pamphlets, and disturbing low-type movie shows. Gortz and his step-brother decide for the more limited but directly effective personal form of social activity; the latter becomes an eye specialist, the former returns to his estate where the presence of a young and energetic administrator and agriculturist is urgently needed to cope with mounting economic difficulties.

When Gortz returns to East Prussia he takes with him a disgruntled Berlin mechanic and his family; the man has long been out of work and is now to be given a new start in life. Gortz also carries out plans to give the children of his tenants better educational facilities. These and similar good intentions and well-meant actions will be smiled upon, by some as a feeble attempt at Christian charity, by others as an easy way for a rich man to soothe his guilty capitalistic conscience. And we may well ask whether the author has not avoided facing the burning problems of the period by taking to the comfortable refuge of the Eastern plains and forests. Can we be expected to attribute some general validity to the thoughts of a young man who has never known financial worries, and who can well afford to sympathize with suffering mankind because he is always sure of finding a haven at home? Even if he should reach very definite progressive social conclusions, must we not surmise that these will somehow reflect the aristocratic colour of his background? True enough, the novel does not boldly examine the economic basis of civilization, let alone advance practical suggestions for changes. Kramp, like so many other German writers, avoids the question of economic implications to concentrate on the more strictly ethical attitudes he deems necessary for the reformation of society. Once we accept this limitation, however, there is no reason to deprecate the value of his findings. Gortz acts from a genuinely ethical conscience and with a sense of spiritual responsibility that might well inspire and help others to pursue much further the quest for the good life. That he reacts to a particular situation with a strength that comes from personal thought does not really impair the general validity of his ethics.

Certainly the author of this novel goes out of his way to try to win our confidence in the findings of Gortz and his other characters. He uses the safeguards of irony and scepticism in his endeavour to make us feel sure that no hasty conclusions are being drawn. He knows, as this whole generation of novelists seems to know, that human beings are ever inclined to mis-interpret their own actions and emotions. Nietzsche's elucidation of the psychology of human motives has deeply penetrated Kramp's consciousness. "Do you think," one of the characters asks, "that there is any possibility at all of reducing at least our own selves to an intelligible formula, and that we are in a position to say whether our own thoughts and actions are good or bad? Into every good deed I wish to do the devil seems to have mixed a shot of self-love, vanity, greed, revengefulness and other ugly ingredients. Do you belive that we can acquire the ability to distinguish the parts that come from God from those that come from Satan?" Gortz and the activist theology student try to answer the question each in his own way, the former relying on instinct and emotion, and the latter trying to lift the problems of existence into the light of reason and dissect them with the tools of a sharp intellect. Neither of these methods proves equal to the task, though a combination of the two will be.

Kramp's conclusion seems to be that the combination of feeling and reason is seldom achieved in one and the same person, but instead arises in a perfect marriage. Hence the paramount importance of finding the right kind of man or woman. It is, incidentally, this search which in the main provides what epic structure the novel has. For a long time Gortz feels strangely attached to Eva, a mysteriously irrational, demonic young girl, until he makes his way back to a neighbouring farmer's daughter, an old acquaintance of his whose womanly instincts and angelic disposition form the predestined supplement to his more passion-ate temperament. The greatest service this woman can render Gortz is to restore his confidence in a God who is more than a name or a frightening emotional experience. God exists, she tells him, and his essence is love. "The last and decisive truth is God's love—by this I mean God's love for us of which our being in love is but a faint reflection. I have always known that God loves me; this is the whole mystery of my existence." Now, if

God's love is to be extended to us, we must love him in return, not with words and feelings alone, but through our deeds. Gortz awakens to his responsibility towards God and develops, with the help of another admirable woman, his aunt, a keen feeling for the concepts of right and wrong, and especially an abhorrence for that worst crime human beings are apt to commit, the wounding of others. But if the realization of our guilt is the first step to a higher self, the second is not to yield to a morbid fear of being inextricably involved in guilt. Watching his newly-born son, Gortz sums up the wisdom he has found in the following soliloquy: ". . . he shall not waste his strength on mean things, or on lies and trifles, with his beloved ones he shall form a fortress against which the devil will batter his head. He shall gather strength, much manly strength for a just fight. But he shall consider himself too good to commit unjust or cruel deeds. And if in spite of all that you fall into errors and sins, my son, be not afraid. For you must know that it is man's lot to become guilty. Only do not fool yourself, be too proud to make excuses, to yourself or to the world, when your conscience accuses you. Go to your mother and let her tell you of the great secret she once revealed to your father, when the shadows of guilt fell heavily upon his heart. Go to your mother to hear from her that divine love is the foundation of all life."

Not often since the days of Jeremias Gotthelf have we been so emphatically exhorted to trust to the love of women for our salvation. Good women have the power to mediate between God and the world; they, much more than men, are endowed with the gift of sanctifying life. The theme has been taken up by many recent German writers. It almost seems as if a man-dominated world had become exhausted and was now willing to hand over the reins to women, or at least to ask for their urgently needed assistance. The admission of man's inability to cope with modern life alone is made in a number of recent educational novels, notably in an impressive work, *Im Strom,* by the well-known writer on American and Canadian life, A. E. Johann.

The hero of this work, Hans Radmacher, on more than one

occasion taxes our patience to the limit by the arrogance of both his words and his actions. It is not, to be sure, the arrogance of Kurt Eggers, but that of an individual who simply cannot accept graciously his dependence on others, though he has no objection to others depending on him. Politically, however, he is too disarmingly honest (or too infinitely shrewd) ever to be taken in by demagogic tactics. It must have been an affront to the powers that were, at the time the novel appeared, that Hans, the son of a stern Prussian official and a good soldier in the First World War, an intellectual with no sympathies for the Weimar Republic, all of a sudden turns his back on politics and comes to the conclusion that his one and only task is to make money, as much of it as is possible without falling foul of the law. And since marrying the sophisticated, decadent daughter of a bankrupt banker promises to help his career, he thinks as little of going through the ceremony as he does afterwards of collusion to obtain a divorce. To cap his antipathy to Germany he finally boards a ship that is to take him to Canada.

The redeeming features of Radmacher's life are his readiness, finally, to recognize the superior qualities of a fine young woman whose love he previously had done so much to hurt, and the steady though slowly-working influence two other excellent women have had over him. One of these was his mother, the other a chance acquaintance, a middle-aged widowed countess in East Prussia. If the latter two have done much to guide his formal education, his manners and personal habits, the former succeeds in breaking his self-centredness and in making him admit humbly that the love of a woman is the greatest treasure of all and something that must be treated as a sacred trust.

This is the lesson carried forward through hundreds of pages filled with the tense incidents of the war and post-war period; other conclusions there are none. It is possible that the second volume the author promises, in which Radmacher's further experiences are to be recorded, will add (or might have added) to the one and only educational conclusion of the first. As matters stand, we must assume that for the most critical political period

of his life A. E. Johann knows of no better solution than to put
one's own house in order—which is mainly a matter of finding
an intelligent and warm-hearted woman—and then to establish
a new existence in some remote part of a peaceful country. However, even this piece of advice runs counter to all official recom-
mendations. Instances of a similarly independent philosophy can
be cited from other novels.

The life of Thomas Reiker in *Vorabend,* by Peter Hergenbrecht, an unforgettable literary creation of the priestlike type of
young man, comes to an untimely end on the Russian front, in
the First World War. That does not, however, confine the educational significance of the book to pre-war conditions, at least not
in the opinion of the author whose hope it must have been that
the philosophy of his hero was timeless enough to be taken over
by those who survived this world war and were called to shape
the future of Germany. Students of Thomas Mann's *Zauberberg*
will recall that the discussions carried on by Castorp, Settembrini,
Naphta, and others relate much more to the period after the war
than to the pre-war setting in which they take place. Hergenbrecht attempts to find solutions that will be valid for years to
come, not just for the decade in which they were evolved. Hence
the solemn presentation of his findings. These are mainly the
result of searching conversations among groups of thoughtful
men and women, for whom the life of the soul remains an
irrefutable reality and one of the principal concerns of human
existence. What suspense the novel creates stems much more
from the inner struggles of the characters than from their out-
ward experiences.

How close the author was to the Stefan George circle it is difficult to judge; the novel indicates attraction to and repulsion
from George. A common background is unmistakeably present:
the Rhineland with its dual tradition from the Roman and the
Catholic heritage; the eager absorption of beauty in all its
manifestations—landscape, architecture, women, manners, and,
not least, literary form. At the same time Hergenbrecht in no
uncertain words declares his disagreement with George's philo-

sophy, or with any other kind of aristocratic aloofness for that matter. In the house of his uncle, a Catholic priest, Thomas reads a few George poems—a song about Mary and the complaint of a father whose son is leaving him to experience the life of an errant knight. The priest acknowledges the great qualities of the poems, and the beautiful image of men they create or celebrate; they are excellent, so far as their deification of man is concerned. "But this is of no real significance for us." In the ensuing discussion, and indeed throughout his life, Thomas is to learn that we are above all called to cope with social and political problems and with spiritual dilemmas; to solve these, and so to realize the highest possibilities of existence, more than the deification of self is needed; we must acquire the ability to face reality courageously. Society as we know it today is fast disintegrating; the value of man has been brought down to the price put on material goods. "Is it not true," the priest again asks, "that [as a consequence of our sophistication] a lover strikes one as a malicious fool? Children are encouraged to get rid of their noblest endowment, of the urge to search for and to revere a higher being." Firmly but with no undue haste the priest tries to kindle in his nephew respect for a Christian tradition which, in the form of Christian humanism, may be brought to bear on modern problems. "This revitalization of our religion is, however, no easy task, and is not something that can be entrusted to liberalistic talkers. There are reasons for grave apprehension; perhaps it is too late for mankind to recapture the meaning of true Christianity, and to rediscover in Christ the teacher who will show us how to distinguish between Good and Evil and who wants us to transcend our material, vegetative constitution, so that we may reach intellectual clarity and spiritual strength. Often it appears to me that we are about to return to the Catacombs. Or will Christ emigrate to other people?"

Thomas is exposed to other than religious inspiration as well —to art, science, social life, and, during his university years, to economics; yet the influence of his uncle remains decisive in the development of his own individual interests. One of these leads him to a study of the social problem of the period, the conditions under which factory workers have to spend their lives. The slum districts of the large cities challenge his will to do something and compel him to at least the promise of future action. In his opinion, one of the principal needs is that there must be some assurance that children from the lower classes will stand as good a chance as others of growing up to be members of one of the important social layers of the future. The same clear realization that changes in the social structure of the period are overdue enables Thomas to see much good in the civilization of the United States where he has spent a few months. He is in love with America, his fiancée claims. Nor does he deny it: "Truly, Eva Maria, it is over there that a new world is arising. The future of that country can hardly be over-estimated. On the surface it looks as if they were merely continuing where we left off. But they are making a fresh start, just as we did a thousand years ago."

Participation in the war reduces the scope of Thomas Reiker's interests, though not the spiritual strength surging through him, his humility and obedience, his comradeship and love. That his author-creator did not allow him to survive the war and to take part in the reconstruction of Germany after 1918 we can understand. The message is all there, its meaning clear and its practical application mapped out for decades to come: love of man in a direct, neighbourly sense. We feel that Thomas would have sacrificed himself after the war in the same manner as he did during the war, for this seemingly small cause, to save somebody's soul and life. For Christianity, and even Christian humanism, is a slow-working process. It is not something that will shake the world today or tomorrow, but a force transforming the world by imperceptible stages, encouraging a sacrificially pure life here, serving as an exhortation to truth and goodwill there; this is all the world will see of the reawakening of Christianity. Hergenbrecht's reaction to the immediate problems of the period after 1918 is one of patience and metaphysical confidence, an attitude not unlike the long-range view of the early Christians. While he does not ignore the political problems of the day, he sees them as conditions that must not be allowed to monopolize our attention.

Other authors likewise treat contemporary political concerns as of passing significance when seen in the light of vital human interests, though these are not necessarily the religious and metaphysical interests of Hergenbrecht.

In a postscript to his novel *Hans Undög,* the author, Johannes Martin Schupp, briefly discusses his literary works in their relation to the times. He mentions among other books of his a novel, *Ebbe und Flut,* the title of which obviously refers to the low tide, economically speaking, that followed the Treaty of Versailles, and to the high tide of a new prosperity and moral regeneration that came with National Socialism. Not having seen the book the writer cannot state how closely it is hewn to party lines. Does it prepare for another low tide, in accordance with the nature symbol of the title? Certainly in *Hans Undög* Schupp makes no mention of the so-called deliverance of Germany, though it must have occurred during the lifetime of his hero. Instead, he confines himself to two perennial experiences of youth: school and first love. Reunited with the girl he loved, lost, and found again, and on the threshold of the university we leave Hans Undög. It is too early to know how he will face subsequent contacts with the world around him. Indications are that he will give a good account of himself, which makes us regret all the more that the author did not go on with his story. Does he stop at this important juncture because he did not feel free to depict the older Hans as he might have been expected to develop, if past experience and the preparation he has had mean anything? Are readers expected to extend the line of his life into the future, and to draw their own conclusions—conclusions such that they could not be made public? Whatever the explanation may be, *Hans Undög* seems to be yet another instance of an author saying as much as he can say with impunity about the need for sympathetic understanding, good intentions, and freedom of development. It may well be that future historians of

German literature will discover among the novelists writing under National Socialist surveillance a very common tendency to avoid a frank encounter with their political masters, and to break off or veer to the side for reasons of self-preservation.

Somewhere in this novel a casual remark is made that one cannot trifle with feelings as one can with thoughts. The statement fits the life of Undög, as it probably fits most adolescents. They have little to say that relates to the realm of thought, depending as they do on their teachers, but they know emotions which they take extremely seriously. Undög's wishful feelings, as we might well call the high expectations of his emotional soul, reach, first for a universe that is meaningful and responsive to his idealistic conceptions, and secondly for a relationship with at least one other human being in which mutual truthfulness and faithfulness can be relied upon. The world, however, is seldom willing to comply with such wishes. Undög draws heavily on his teachers and on books and friends in order to have his emotional anticipation of a purposeful world corroborated by the knowledge of older people. There are, of course, a number of petrified elders, teachers especially, who offer him stones instead of bread and threaten to turn him into a cynic. On the whole, however, he is fortunate in getting encouragement for his *a priori* belief that man embodies the highest manifestation of cosmic energy. Though only a tiny speck in the universe, man possesses the ability to reflect on what he is and what he ought to become. "We feel that God is above man and the earth below him, and man's ambition it is to strive upward. Now if the whole visible world is made of the same essence as man, then the world is irresistibly moving from earth to heaven, from matter to God."

To one so eager as Hans Undög to have his ethical beliefs moored in absolute certainty, no greater gift could have come than the impromptu speech of one of his teachers who drops in at the matriculation party of Undög's class. "The experience of life has taught mankind to distinguish between virtues and vices. Virtue helps to build up society, while vice will destroy it. Only those noble promptings which we really possess and which cannot be pretended prove to be the invincible forces of growth and the defence of mankind. Love is the spur of courage, lust the net of cowardice. Where this net chokes noble instincts and deprives them of their strength, art will fade away, knowledge wither, customs, peoples, and nations disintegrate. The call of love is the clarion call to mankind. Love is in us, just as intelligence and blood are in us, imperishable all of them. Goethe has expressed their categorical imperative: Let man be noble, helpful, and good. The obligation of man towards himself entails at the same time his highest obligation towards society. More eternal and imperishable than all forms is a country founded on love. . . ."

Undög can leave school and enter university with a philosophy of life in which the heritage of Goethe, Christ, Zoroaster, Plato quickens his own fervent hopes and stirrings. Farther than that the author does not or dare not take us, much as the reader would like to penetrate into the realm of adult life in order to see the practical working out of Undög's lofty intentions.

Those who take an interest in Undög's rather inconclusive experiences as a young lover have equal reason to wonder: what now? The last we see of Hans is a scene of reconciliation, with kisses and the exchange of mutual vows for eternal love, a lofty promise for two so young. The love episodes, while they do not significantly affect the intellectual and spiritual growth of the hero, bring to mind a dilemma of which many an adolescent boy has painful memories. The young girls whose skates they fasten with trembling hands, and with whom they discuss Buddha, Plato, and the migration of the soul, soon find out that they are old enough to attract the attention of men with more serious intentions, who are in a position to marry them. The romance of Hans Undög is interrupted by the appearance of just such a man, a young high-school teacher, who can talk about and afford the price of an engagement ring. Fortunately for Hans the rival does not press his advantage strongly enough; once again reality complies with his emotional ideals, by reuniting him with the one and only girl he can love.

If we except *Axel Horn* and *Das innere Bild*—and the two

exceptions do not count for very much—the leading characters of recent German educational novels are all eager to climb the steps to higher education. They go through the gymnasium, and, if possible, through the university. The institutions of higher learning cannot, of course, perform miracles. Eggers, as we have seen, does not gain in the least from his contact with the theological faculty, and the others keenly feel the need to supplement their academic training by what experience they can gather from the agitated stream of life. Even so, there is every evidence that higher learning holds a central position in their endeavour to form a philosophy of existence. And for one of them, for Maurus Munk, in *Maurus und sein Turm,* by Franz K. Franchy, the university is a sacred symbol of all that makes life worth living; it is a tower sending forth knowledge. "The sounds ringing from it should be like bells exhorting us to watchfulness, justice, and love. Blessed be the country where such towers stand, blessed the country that shows itself worthy of them."

The courses Maurus takes are the time-honoured subjects of the humanities: linguistic studies, history of literature, philosophy and ethics. Nothing is said of the modern scientific trend, nor has he a motive for study other than that of expanding the range of his knowledge as a means of understanding himself and the world around him. If he is mature enough to appreciate the intrinsic value of the humanities, it is probably because for many years in his youth he had to go without the help of education. At the threshold of the upper classes in the local gymnasium he was forced to leave school and start an apprenticeship with a watchmaker, his father's fortune having been diminished as a result of the actions of a dishonest bookkeeper. Maurus's youth becomes overburdened with the experience of social ostracism and economic dependency and with the sorrow of being misunderstood and left to brood. Driven within himself he grows accustomed to a life of intense introspection, with only an occasional sortie into the outside world. This, we presume, predestines Maurus to associate with a strange mentor, a retired school-teacher whose educational philosophy, hitherto wasted on thoughtless youth, now finds an eager disciple. Kilian Vogt teaches Maurus to persevere in his ambition to lead an ethically sound life, at the same time advising him not to be unduly alarmed about the fact that the common run of men are materialistic and brutally acquisitive. For base striving will often end in disappointment, and out of disappointment many a man will awake to the realization of a higher existence and become susceptible to the message of true teachers. Even wicked men are seldom beyond hope. "What does life require? Love! Can love be taught? It ought to be taught. It is a case of finding man in his pit of despair."

Here again, as so often in recent German educational novels, such inner riches seem to accumulate without being useful to society, or without reference to economic problems. It is questionable whether Maurus, with all his ability to draw satisfaction from intellectual and spiritual pursuits, would be able to make a living, or even marry the girl he loves and establish his own home. A veritable *deus ex machina* has to be brought into action to provide for his material needs, and for some of his intellectual needs as well. Maurus comes into possession of a great fortune, through a belated act of restitution on the part of the man who once ruined his father. But if fate had not made this good investment for him, who would have done it? What good would Kilian Vogt's mentorship have been to him, if he had remained poor? The question indicates a serious flaw which none of these novelists seem to be able to avoid. Education should include guidance in the ethical acquisition of the wherewithal for a livelihood, instead of ignoring such material needs or depending on their being satisfied from the pocket of a rich father or, as in the case of Maurus, by some sort of magic trick.

Moreover, no educational philosophy will appeal to our generation unless it expresses a definite attitude towards social and economic concerns. This demand was not made of the novels of the eighteenth and early nineteenth centuries, either because the readers of those days still had an unshaken confidence in the permanency of a pseudo-feudal order which would always provide for the privileged classes, or because they too believed in a strict dualism of spiritual and material life. The modern world will accept neither of these points of view, and looks askance at a third possible attitude which advocates acceptance of whatever social conditions happen to prevail and muddling through as best one can. The challenge of social injustice and misery is such that any writer who ignores it cannot be considered really significant, no matter how engaging his work may be in content or in form.

We can, then, criticize recent German educational novels, that is, those that have a serious claim on our attention, for not being boldly explicit on the social situation and instead accepting and perpetuating the dualistic conception of an inner and an outer life. Liberals and idealists have, of course, at all times been fond of thinking that spiritual effort as such will in due time affect and mitigate the material shortcomings of existence. It is true, too, that there has been in the educational novels under discussion an impressive harvest of intellectual and spiritual truths. Perhaps this was all these authors could accomplish, hindered as they must have been in any attempt to draw the complementary social, political, and economic conclusions. However, the future will have to show whether such reluctance was really the result of official *force majeure* only, or whether it arose partly also from that strong romantic tradition that has done so much, in Germany, to keep thought and action, imagination and reality separate from one another.

7 Foreign Countries

IN THE study of novels in any literature the question as to how foreign countries fare is not ordinarily one that imperatively presents itself. It does so, however, in times of fervent political activity when national characteristics become a topic of acute interest.

There is another reason for inserting a short chapter on the treatment of foreign countries. Contrary to expectation, not all recent German novels which take us into foreign lands are tainted with a preconceived bias or soaked with propaganda. Against a background of rubbish there stand out a small number of works that must have infuriated chauvinistic simpletons, by virtue of their intellectual honesty and fair-mindedness towards the political and military enemies of Germany.

Rudolf Michael's *Roman einer Weltreise,* the report of a world tour arranged for a number of German newspapermen, does not properly fall within the scope of this survey, despite its title. As background material, however, it is very handy, presenting as it does an officially sanctioned political picture of global dimensions. For on this journey that takes him from Italy to Port Said, and thence to Colombo, Singapore, Hongkong, Japan, Peiping, Hawaii and through the United States, the author sees only what he was prepared to see or asked to see. His comments amount to little more than a post-factum confirmation of the official line on political and ethnical problems. The sole theme is that of the inevitable ascendancy of the totalitarians over the Anglo-Saxons, above all over the English. Sailing in European waters he sees England's influence everywhere and asks: "Is England really a European power? Her memories lie in England, her hopes are with Canada, her money in Suez, her ships in

Singapore. All she wants in Europe is peace, peace for a lazy nation. Contented nations are always opposed to motion." As Michael traverses the Far Eastern zones he gathers comforting evidence from Germans living in diaspora and from their consular representatives. "A strange thing, this myth of English invincibility. As long as a nation is smart enough not to court danger and to produce the semblance of working for peace, the world will believe in its invincibility. But woe, if fate should one day insist on seeing definite proof of such pretended strength."

It is annoying to see the opportunities offered by this beautiful trip wasted upon one who can never detach himself from preconceived ideas. The book, however, becomes more pathetic than annoying when our traveller is taken in by a revelation like the following, attributed to the proverbial resident of long standing, a fictitious person, we presume, who serves now and then as the author's mouthpiece: "You mean that the Chinese haven't enough national feeling?" "At least not in the European sense of willingness for self-sacrifice, absolute surrender, dynamism, and heroism. The Chinese are by instinct deeply fond of their country. But their heroism is of a passive nature. History often has shown them to possess such heroism abundantly; the passive suffering of the people has overcome abysmal calamities. But will this suffice in modern times? Even now, 80,000 Chinese regulars are fighting on the side of the Japanese. Telling symptoms: the Japanese are dynamic and heroic; on these qualities they base their claims in the Far East. The world belongs to the courageous one." Crossing the Pacific Ocean from Japan to the United States, the author is soon able to state the basic difference between the two nations: the land of the rising sun is all virility, whereas the Americans show many irrefutable indications of decadence, such as mass meetings for freedom, tolerance, and peace, with only the occasional rally against the Jews to redress the balance. It is a sad spectacle to see a man whose calling it is to mould public opinion stuck in such a morass of prejudices and snap judgments.

This and other similarly distorted pictures of the political world can be conveniently dismissed as the hasty impressions of travellers who have neither the time nor the patience nor the knowledge to enter the countries they describe in any other than a physical sense. Yet those who have lived long in some foreign country have also made fools of themselves when writing about the affairs of their adopted land. The contempt bred by this kind of familiarity provides interesting psychological material and suggests, in some instances, a subtle form of schizophrenia. Love and hatred for the adopted land balance one another until some incident, quite often a very trivial one, tips the scales. Unaccountable malice leads to constant fault-finding with the adopted country and to the glorification of the good old homeland, both attitudes being reversed when the old land is in sight again.

Hans Kitzinger in his autobiographical novel *Die Farm am Erongo* presents no such psychological puzzle. If he ever loved the hills of German South-West Africa, even in retrospect, he certainly does not admit it. He was perhaps cut out to become a successful farmer in this German colony, but the First World War interfered with his plans and led to internment, the loss of his farm and cattle, and another start from scratch followed by more evictions and ultimately by the fruitless attempt to collect indemnities from the Weimar Republic. Out of these and other harrowing experiences Kitzinger fashions a bitter tale. His bitterness is however not that of an African Job; ill luck has made him sour, pusillanimous, and unjust in his ever ready condemnation of the English and the Boers. A wiser and more mature man, even if he were unable to laugh off all this bad luck, might have distilled from it a philosophy of pessimism, or have learned to view things with equanimity and contemplation. Kitzinger has acquired none of these attitudes; he is a conceited braggart, always asking for trouble with his brazen *Deutschland über Alles* impudence. At no point is he ever capable of describing his misfortunes in the spirit of the happy-go-lucky adventurer. It is possible that the absence of humour and sympathy may be due to the advanced age at which this farmer turned author but it is more likely that he never had any trace of either.

The resilience of youth after hardships accounts for another, more attractive type of settler novel, two representatives of which take us to Canada. Ilse Schreiber (*Die Flucht ins Paradies*) writes about an obviously self-experienced struggle to leave the hinterland and to gain a foothold in city life. Lothar Matthaei (*Irgendwo drüben in Kanada*) has no other ambition than to roam through the length and breadth of the Canadian expanse, and to keep alive as best he can. He calls his book an adventurous report, a title that is well earned. Both authors had to contend with the depression after 1929 which seems to keep abreast of them no matter where they turn. Yet such is their wholesome joy in being alive and in meeting the challenge of a coldly apathetic world that, instead of growing disgruntled, they draw an increasing inner strength from their adversities. Matthaei, more factual, and tongue-tied when it comes to subjective confessions, shows his mettle by a never failing resourcefulness and by an ability to adapt himself to the exigencies of a turbulent struggle for survival. The very absence of nationalistic nonsense and sentimentality reveals the growth, deep in his soul, of that rough-hewn cosmopolitanism which develops in lumber camps, on the wheat fields of the prairie, and in the employment offices and poolrooms of the cities. Ilse Schreiber has a way of embedding in her epic material, from time to time, layers of emotion and reflection, and critical pronouncements on life in general or on Canada in particular. Her observations on Canada show none of the malice bred by lack of success, but rather sincere appreciation, as when she speaks of the deep-seated longing in almost all Canadian hearts to draw into the material comforts of their lives a more spiritual leaven. Though she has to return to the small farm from which she set out, she feels the satisfaction of having brought home something extremely beautiful, a new zest for life.

Neither she nor Matthaei has any political design on the country they have chosen to live in. To be sure, they meet other Germans and exchange reminiscences of the old country or form friendships, but this is natural and as it should be. At the end of his story we see Matthaei trekking away from a small town into the grey distance, with a companion, also a German. They march not to conquer the world but to find a job, and, even more urgent, to get something to eat. It is regrettable that Ilse Schreiber's account ends with a patriotic flourish (Canada becoming the fatherland of many Germans, and the native paradise of their hearts for which they are longing) that is not in keeping with the broadly human atmosphere of the rest of the book. Did she think that some such lyrical effusion was necessary to make the book acceptable to the publisher and safe on German book-shelves?

It is hard to say, with no other evidence than his book, whether O. E. H. Becker ever was in Australia. Little is said in *Das australische Abenteuer* about present-day conditions of Aus-tralian life that an imaginative mind could not glean from secondary sources, and there is much in it which he could only have collected from printed records no matter how long he might have lived in the country. For the "Australian Adventure" is not really a narrative centring on one particular character; it is the history of Australia as reflected in the experiences of early immigrants who settled, or rather were forced to settle, there. A most interesting anthology of stories this is; the framework has strong merits of its own, but it is the numerous bits of historical information contributed by old settlers and told to the young German immigrant that raise the work to the level of Sealsfield's American stories. What happens to Becker as he penetrates into remote ranching districts is all very instructive and makes us desirous of knowing more about this continent. To grant our wish the author then takes us back into earlier days, to a time in England when unfortunate men and women, labelled criminals for some misdemeanour which today would be thrashed out be-fore a juvenile court or a justice of the peace, were given harsh sentences, afterwards commuted to deportation to Australia, where they have to earn complete freedom in long years of semi-servitude.

For a foreigner like Becker this record of brutality presents tempting opportunities for criticism. He neither excuses the brutality of the past nor condones the ruthlessness of the present, though he realizes that out of the sufferings of thousands of people the genius of England for colonization was enabled to join a great continent to her own Western civilization. "What comfort is it to know that the Germans, in many ways, are superior to the British, who lack the persistency of the Germans, their faithfulness and reliability, their sense of justice, their love of the soil? The fact remains that the British have created an empire, leaving the Germans to enumerate the points wherein they surpass other nations." But Becker's admiration is magnanimous and free from envy. It comes as no surprise that he decides to stay in Australia and to become part of the great adventure. He has every right to do so, having given proof that he should be considered a desirable immigrant, by his general frame of mind and by his having hunted down a long-sought criminal, which enables an innocent prisoner to gain his freedom.

It is rare to find as much love and admiration for the Anglo-Saxon scene as Becker has, without any of the usual fretting reaction of jealousy that leads to left-handed compliments, to fault-finding, and to the declaration of German superiority, in some form or other. Becker may simply have a disposition that takes naturally to life in the free open spaces. The more significant test comes, of course, when we turn to professional writers, that is to men who, it is assumed, have their sensibilities developed beyond the measure of ordinary mortals, and are cognizant of a responsibility towards their fellow-men, whose opinions they try to influence.

To consider first the material relating to Anglo-Saxon countries would seem natural in view of the fact that German literature, autobiographical and imaginative, shows a definite preoccupation with English and above all with American life. True enough, a large number of the books within the scope of this survey deal with other European countries. Upon Italy, for instance, is bestowed an attention the like of which it has not received since the late eighteenth century. But it is no exaggeration to say that the aspect under which modern Italians are seen is uninteresting in the extreme, even where the picture does not simply follow the official version of the heroic Axis partner and the revival of ancient Rome. The English, and equally the Americans, are, on the other hand, a perpetual challenge to the Germans, who find themselves tossed about by a whirl of emotional cross-currents whenever they meet an Anglo-Saxon. The Americans they call childish, simple, crudely materialistic, *Motorenmenschen* (to use an expression coined by Finckenstein) —and yet they would like to share their bath-tub civilization. The English they abuse with all sorts of names: hypocrites, utilitarians, European Chinese—yet they envy them all the while because they get along at home and with other nations.

How are we to explain the fact that some recent German authors go out of their way to give the Anglo-Saxons their due recognition? Was it because such praise offered one last outlet for their annoyance with a press and government propaganda that constantly insulted their intelligence and tried to break their integrity? The absolute impartiality, for instance, with which von Simpson in his generation novels of the Barrings, *Die Barrings* and *Der Enkel*, treats the English cousins of that family must have been irritating to a German reader who would expect to see at least an occasional reference to the perfidy of Albion, to the snobbishness of her aristocracy, and to the insidious conspiracy of rich and poor in England to rob hard-working foreigners of the fruits of their labour. Von Simpson never makes even an inadvertent slip in the direction of such popular conceptions, which is evidence of his ingrained fairness and will to objectivity. He is continuing in the tradition of Fontane and it is gratifying to see that he has inherited the spirit as well as the technical ability of his predecessor. The only thing to be regretted, in this connexion, is the fact that his English scene pictures the upper classes only and leaves out the lower social stratum.

The substance of von Simpson's novels lies outside the scope of this chapter, however.[1] Another author, Erich Ebermayer, indicates in the very title of his novel *Unter anderm Himmel,* "Under a Different Sky," an ethnographic bent. It is a blatantly

[1]See chapter I.

distorted performance, a disappointing record from a man who spent his formative years in the intellectually stimulating climate of the Weimar Republic. This book on American life should have a calamitous effect upon the author's reputation and relegate him to the company of Courts-Mahler. It brings before us an immensely rich Wall Street magnate, in his office an awe-inspiring demi-god but a silly lamb and a trembling leaf at home; his wife, who feels only hatred for her pretty daughter; and this daughter, who falls in love at first sight with the newly engaged accountant, an officer recently returned from the war. Around these and other caricatures is built a plot in which everybody soon has to hire a private detective, and, as if this was not enough to interest a second-rate movie producer, the author adds a sentimental attachment of the young girl for a finishing school at Heidelberg. Her intense longing for Germany reveals itself to be the bequest from her real father, an itinerant German baritone with whom her mother had had a love affair before marrying the banker. No attention need have been paid to this work here but for the fact that its author was once considered a promising and progressive German novelist. Obviously something more than talent is needed, in times of intellectual corruption, to keep the level of imaginative integrity high. Indeed Ebermayer's case is, considered in another way, highly instructive; for his failure to recreate the American scene results, in the final analysis, from the combination of a lack of understanding with this superficial talent. A good writer is synonymous either with a good observer, or with a clear thinker, or with an emotionally sensitive personality. If an author can be all these, so much the better! But even if he is only one of them, he cannot possibly produce nothing except clichés. He may and probably will be much better at analysing his own countrymen than other nationals; but knowing his own people he will never write such rank nonsense about others as Ebermayer does.

It is equally sad to see that A. E. Johann, with a fine novel *Im Strom* (see chapter VI) to his credit, has allowed considerations of easy popularity to interfere with his natural bent, which was and still is to love the New World. When he published his first book on his Canadian journey he was the never-to-be-downed young man filled with a zest for life that made good use of every experience, hardships and all. In a more recent book, *Das Land ohne Herz,* on the United States, in which he hops hither and thither along the Canadian-American border, he knows of only one purpose, to convince his countrymen that the United States is on the verge of an economic and moral collapse from which there is no escape. Farms that have been allowed to drift away in sandstorms; artists starving in basement dwellings; people living in trailers and beginning to like it, so that they become incapacitated for normal living—these are the characteristics of America he now discovers. His visit to the United States took place in the early thirties and coincided with the depression; what he saw was a few berries from *The Grapes of Wrath.* The misery and hopelessness of these and other years are, of course, undeniable facts, but the reaction they evoke in him remains peculiarly subjective, a mixture of pity and *Schadenfreude,* and they are a pretext to denounce everything. He knows much about the neglect and the exploitation that have brought about inhuman conditions, but he has no experience of the currents of sympathy and of social responsibility stirring among many Americans. His attitude is not one that comes natural to young people, who are usually generous. "The Country without a Heart" meets the Third Reich propaganda more than half-way.

The sad part about this performance is that Johann once knew better, and that even now he has to admit a deep-seated love for America. "I know no land under the sun, except my own country, which I love as much as I love America." This confession is the residue of his former impressions. To account for his change of heart from love to hatred, he advances a puerile excuse: he dislikes what he once loved because the Americans have not lived up to his expectations; they have thrown away God's most munificent gifts; they have failed to cultivate their forests and to look after their fertile prairies. If there was once a time in which the free, manly spirit of the pioneers was given scope to develop, such a time has long passed and given way to one of ruthless abuse and irretrievable disintegration. "It was not the intention of this book to discuss whether America can win the war or whether she must lose it. But I have perhaps been able to make clear . . . that this American system does not deserve to win the war and to expand over the rest of the world, and that it is not worth our while to try to find in the conditions of American life something desirable, either for the Germans or for Europe in general." To have known America as Johann once did, when he delighted in her vitality, optimism, buoyancy, and warm-hearted sympathies, and then all of a sudden to deny such knowledge, is a very shocking spectacle when we reflect on its deeper implications, for it involves the wanton pollution of a source from which nothing but the truth should flow.

There is only one way of finding out how foreign countries and their inhabitants think, act, and feel, and that is by living among them, if not forever, at least for a longer time than wandering scribes of all nations can usually spend. Creative writing takes cognizance of this fact when it explores other nations, especially the United States, by means of immigrant characters. Stories of immigrants follow, as a rule, one of two possible courses: the immigrant will either be made to stay, or he will, after some time, be returned to the place he came from, a wiser man, or a more disgruntled one.

Franz Brennert, the hero of an immigrant novel by Arthur E. Grix, *Umweg über Frisco,* does not come of his own free will to the United States. This young Berlin student gets into trouble, politically, by taking an inconspicuous part in the revolution of 1848, and emotionally, by falling in love with a pretty dancer. These are sufficient reasons for a middle-class father to arrange for his passage to New York, where the lad is to work in the firm of a business friend. But ere long he succumbs to the lure of the Western spaces and he finally reaches the gold fields of California. There comes a time when he no longer thinks of returning to Germany, and his decision to leave America is more the result of a sudden emotional impulse than of forethought and preparation.

What impressions does he take home? Is American life to be

understood as a rampant form of materialism, as he was on occasion inclined to believe? Or can it be trusted to lead in time to a high cultural level? Brennert does not discuss these and other problems with any great degree of intellectual acumen, but solves them pragmatically, by loving America. After a first and natural period of bewilderment and hesitancy, he had made up his mind to survive instead of sinking into the sea of nostalgic dreams. However, he fitted into the pioneering caravans without giving up his good German heritage. When at times the urge to sing and play the guitar became irresistible, he drew equally from American and from German folk-lore. So, when he returns to Germany, the New World loses a good prospective citizen, while Germany gains a man of considerable *Weltoffenheit* who can be counted on to stand up for the Americans. The stagnant waters from which Franz escaped in 1848 have not all receded at the time of his homecoming; there is a great need for courageous, independent citizens, and he can help to fill that need. If the author of this novel intended to snub contemporary official propaganda and its anti-American line, he carried out his intentions without taking elaborate safeguards. The camouflage of a mildly historical setting will deceive no one.

Hermann Strenger in a brief epilogue to his novel *Strom aus der Erde* tells us that his imagination was guided by the life of the chemist Hermann Frasch, who as a young man migrated to the United States, to become the American oil king after much hard work and by virtue of his scientific training and inventive genius. The revelation that biographical material underlies this truly outstanding novel comes as a surprise. The external events, it is true, in spite of their exciting nature and realistic presentation, a modern author could have invented or compiled from available sources of information. The inner life, on the other hand, is so rich, intelligent, and human that only the heightened sensibilities of a poet could have experienced it; the author must have added much, if not most of it, from his own resources.

To indicate the measure of the mental reserves the author possesses, one has but to say that young Hermann, the hero of the story, before leaving his Swabian town has already lived through 150 pages of youthful existence sparkling with vitality and filled with intellectual promise and ethical effort, yet does not arrive in Boston a tired or disappointed man whose further inner development could be told briefly (no matter how exciting his exterior adventures might sound). On the contrary, Hermann is as alert on foreign soil as he was in his native surroundings, and as eager to use all his abilities, emotional and intellectual. Another 400 pages are needed to tell of his life in America. True enough, many of these are filled with descriptive material, as is to be expected considering the drastic change of scene from a quaint German small town to the new continent. Even so, the process of his mental and spiritual development is never left unregarded for long, and, while not all the relevant problems may have been touched, the fact remains that Strenger probes deeper into immigrant psychology than any other German author.

Hermann has a complex character, and because of this he also tends to create complex patterns of behaviour in others. Having a variety of instincts to satisfy, he is driven to participate in many spheres of activity, business, art, science, and politics. His scientific interests are almost matched by his aesthetic tastes; he turns Bohemian at times, and then again becomes a strict disciplinarian, at least with himself. There is little or nothing in him of the negative attitude which newcomers often display. Upon coming to America he falls in love with both the fascinating independence of her women and the adventurous spirit of her men in industry and in applied science. Though the author does not allow him to become a sentimentalist, neither is he willing to let him harden into a cold-blooded, successful self-made man. In what activities, then, can he properly release his vitality?

The characters hovering around him answer this question, at least in part. There is his uncle, a professor of chemistry who has close contacts with industry and research, a zealous worker alive only in his laboratory. Outside of it he merely vegetates, going through the paces of family life without much emotional attachment. There is Jan, a combination of siren and business woman,

a vampire using the charms of her body and the gifts of an unusual brain to extract financial and technical information from
her friends and competitors. Hermann is conscious of an elective
affinity for both these personalities, but feels he must reconcile
this attraction with his strong ethical bent. How can a woman,
so he asks himself, emerge all of a sudden out of the tempest of
her emotions and soberly put aside the ecstatic abandon to erotic
union, to talk about real estate, the stock market, and the price
of cotton? But had he not himself been listening with great attention to such topics, while holding her in his arms? One way in
which he manages to break up this disgusting symbiosis of eros
and business is by applying his warm feelings and his keen intellect
to a higher task. This higher task is outlined by his developing
social responsibilities which provide for his talents a wider and
more dignified scope. When visiting Sicily he is faced with the
sad reverse of his own good fortunes; the production of Louisiana
sulphur which his inventions have made possible and turned into
a very lucrative business has resulted in a sharp decline in the
demand for Sicilian sulphur. As usual, the workers have to bear
the brunt of the slump. Hermann takes the plight of these proletarians into consideration and proposes to divide the markets
with the Anglo-Saxon company. "He was the last man to seize
the elements, cunningly, in order to push men into misery. It
was not his intention to extract something from the bowels of the
earth, only to let it break through the dams and destroy all
human values. His science was not to lose all deeper meaning.
He considered it the duty of the human mind to solve the one
great problem: that of bringing order into chaos, of harnessing
the latter after having conquered it. The greater our intellectual
power becomes, the wider the range of its application, the more
urgent our duty to make good use of it and to control these
powers for the benefit of humanity."

The volcanic soil of Sicily is symbolic of Hermann's character
which is in the habit, from time to time, of throwing out its streams
of fiery passions. But if he does make mistakes he never becomes
small-minded or lacks generosity. He has had experience of "the

vermin of the world"; but he also knows that the unrelenting effort of a striving soul can do much to make life bearable, individually and collectively. The American scene of the last century offered to a dynamic personality such as his opportunities, the like of which no other country has provided, to apply his visions to great tasks, to satisfy his quest for richness of experience, and to work off his polemic instincts by attacking the spokesmen of untrammelled materialism. A psycho-analyst might well be tempted to regard the hero of this and similar German-American stories as the fulfilment of the wish for a richer life than that offered by a class-ridden Europe. It is a dream which has come true in thousands of instances.

As a confession of longing for and love of America Strenger's novel cannot have failed to stir a yearning in Germans for a country which enables man to exercise his best faculties to the full; what makes the attraction all the more irresistible is the fact that Hermann remains proudly conscious of his German origin and of the contribution other Germans have made to American civilization, though he does not ask for any other privilege than that of being accepted as an American by other Americans. On his visit to his native town in Germany nobody dares to take old Hermann to task for having become a good American; as one of the speakers at the reunion banquet puts it, a truly useful achievement, made abroad, will enhance the reputation of Germany and continue to bear fruit. Significantly enough all of Hermann's friends, old and new, dwell on his generosity and kindness as his finest qualities.

The achievement of his life is recorded in his deeds rather than in a string of clever utterances; yet his final realization that a new stage has been reached by mankind, or at least by men who have spent years in an Anglo-Saxon country and who have come to value the conception of order within freedom, though slowly developed by Strenger, is worked out with sufficient emphasis for a careful reader.

The United States invariably will draw out a European author; the same cannot be said of South America, judging from the novels available dealing with life in South American states. There is no need to give more than a few samples. Joseph M. Velter (*Unruhig ist unser Herz*) uses a Guatemalan plantation mainly as a retreat for a German violinist; the remote place helps to solve his personal problem: like Tonio Kröger, he yearns for normal, ordinary life. Georg Elert (*Gastspiel in Chiriqui*) repeats an old story, the ravages wrought upon men by alcoholic indulgence; not the slightest attempt is made to enter into the psychology of a foreign people. Wilhelm Wirbitzky (*In zwei Welten*) takes us with an immigrant couple to southern Brazil, into a colony of German settlers. The colony is, however, hermetically sealed against the outside world, and little as we hear about the social and economic problems of the settlers, we learn much less of the indigenous population; in the enclave it is thus possible to proclaim unswerving loyalty to Germany, to hold secret political meetings, and to air a hatred of the Weimar Republic. Frank E. Christoph (*Sehnsucht nach der Heimat*) has not much good to say about Venezuela, to which country the hero of his novel has been invited to come by a friend, who dies before the newcomer sets foot on land. Lazy negroes, sloppy half-breeds, and Jews taking advantage of penniless greenhorns are his main impressions. The arrival of the hero's fiancée increases his difficulties, and even after their situation begins to improve it is never allowed to grow so comfortable as to make them feel happy and at home. The author—following a well-known pattern of such stories of Germans abroad—uses every device to keep home-sickness acute. As was to be expected, the grouchy couple finally decide to return to their native Austria; there they experience a transition from hell to heaven. For in the meantime (as the pattern prescribes) the *Anschluss* has taken place, everybody is now assured of a decent living, and no German Aryan will ever again be tossed out into an inferior and hostile world. Even a jail term which the hero failed to serve before he left is set aside by a more enlightened judicial system. Here as in similar novels the changes brought about by National Socialism form the *raison d'être* of literary production, and we cannot possibly expect the foreign scene to be described otherwise than as a dark foil.

8 History

HISTORY is the happy hunting-ground for the dilettante writer. Here are to be found ready-made characters and plots; the aura of passion exhaled by certain historical figures and events may easily be passed off as his own emotional strength. The quaint diction of ancient documents enables him to slip into a prefabricated style. Thoughts and controversial issues present themselves without much effort, if he but blows into the dust of history. Some writers, again, mistake the not so rare ability to equip a hero of the past with spoon and fork and to make him talk to servants and coachmen for a life-creating power.

One of the most obvious trends of recent German fiction is just such a flight of literary moths into the candle-light of history. The flight seems to be made indiscriminately into every period. Closer inspection, however, reveals preferences which result in clusters of novels around certain historical characters or turning-points, *Weltwenden,* as these authors read them.

National Socialism, like any other revolutionary movement, has had its devotees who busied themselves with the integration of the past and the present, intending either to show that present achievements have been long prepared in the past or to expose the now silenced opposition as a menace that came near to ruining the whole nation. Novelists find it much easier to take up this business of revaluation than responsible historians do. The latter, if they have not abandoned all integrity, see themselves hemmed in by undeniable facts and documents, by what was actually said or done. True enough, the connecting text allows much opportunity for subjective conjectures, but in comparison with fiction-writers, who merrily jump all barriers, the historians are sluggish pedestrians.

Historical personalities who have been revived in modern

German novels, for the purpose of attesting to the venerable age of a now finally fulfilled political dream, are Moritz von Sachsen, Wallenstein, and, most frequently of all, Prince Eugene of Savoy.[1]

The first of these, Moritz von Sachsen, is a newcomer to this illustrious group of great or near-great German leaders before the appearance of the Leader. Known to students of history as the loyal son-in-law of Philip of Hesse, that staunch supporter of Protestantism whom Charles V held incarcerated, he was one of the principal organizers of the rebellion against the Spanish Hapsburgs which ended with the Passau compromise of 1552 and paved the way for the concessions made to the Protestants in the Passau agreement of 1555.[2] Hans Baumgarten (*Moritz von Sachsen*) seizes the slight opportunity offered by history and proclaims Moritz the foremost opponent of the Spanish intrusion in Germany, which by implication also makes him one of the early advocates of German unity. There are, of course, other incidents which help to sustain the claim for Moritz' early vision of a united Germany—his participation in the war against the Turks, for instance, or his punitive expedition against the Margrave of Brandenburg-Kulmbach who had refused to abide by the Passau articles and threatened to plunge Germany into another internecine war. Despite all these, the author still has to rely more on conjecture than on factual material to support his thesis. Fortunately for the speculative novelist Moritz lost his life at an early age; Baumgarten is therefore free to raise and answer the question of what might have happened had he but lived

[1]Bernd Isemann in *Das härtere Eisen* presents another of these forerunners of the Third Reich, Duke Georg Hans, Count of Lützelstein. But for his early death in 1592, at the age of forty-nine, "he would have been the man to save Germany from the Thirty Years' War and to give the Germans a strong frontier in the West. Alsace and the German parts of Lorraine would have stayed within the Reich. Not even a most sceptical observer of his life will venture to predict at what point his plans might have been stopped." Interesting as Isemann's novel is as a picture of sixteenth-century life, the position of Georg Hans was too insignificant to allow him to be more than one among countless other political day-dreamers.

[2]Paul Koehler recommends for Moritz the cognomen "Der grosse Wettiner" (*Moritz von Sachsen*, 1942).

longer. We are told that he would have become a *Mehrer des Reiches,* in the East, in order to make good the loss of Lorraine for which he was to blame. In due time Moritz might even have aspired to the crown of the German Empire.

The shortness of Moritz' life does not lend credibility to such political plans and historians, with very few exceptions, have never credited him with dreams of a greater and united Germany. A figure like Albrecht von Wallenstein, on the other hand, will meet a nationalistic imagination more than half-way.

No less an historian than Ranke has portrayed Wallenstein as the great visionary whose deepest concern it was to establish the unity of Germandom against all separatist tendencies, whether of Protestant or of Catholic colour. A prefatory note in a new edition of his book on Wallenstein, published in 1942, succinctly contrasts Ranke's high expectations with Wallenstein's failure to live up to them. "In Wallenstein the German soul seems to have found its embodiment, a soul that during the Thirty Years' War deteriorated in the most terrible fashion. Torn, in his youth, between Bohemian Protestantism and strict Catholicism, he worked as a strategist and statesman for the greatness of the Imperial House, and consequently for the greatness of Germany. Yet even he succumbed to the evil desire for vainglorious independence and for the exuberant display of splendour." By his own admission, the editor cannot wholly whitewash Wallenstein. It would indeed be foolish to attempt this in a book which expresses cautious misgivings with regard to Wallenstein's character.

In 1937 there appeared two novels both of which aim at a more lenient view of Wallenstein's personal and military-political record. Gerhart Ellert, quick to realize that the time was propitious for a mixture of historical revaluation and adventure, drew a variety of figures, Michelangelo, Charles V, Gerbert of Aurillac, and Sultan Saladin into his rapid production of novels. His *Wallenstein* reveals a greater power of narrative suspense than of psychological discrimination or historical philosophy. Gerhard Bohlmann's *Wallenstein,* on the other hand, has many engaging features to recommend it, not the least of these being a wise restraint in the application of the popular thesis. Wallenstein here emerges slowly as the advocate of peace, after a period of aimless soldiering. The savagery of war, the slaughter of innocent people on both sides of the line become too much for him; after Regensburg he speaks of a guilty conscience and of a debt which he has to pay, not to the Emperor and not to the Church, but to common men and to the German nation as a whole. It is his soliloquies on these themes (really the thoughts of the novelist) which are then compared with the actual conduct of Wallenstein in his last years, that is, his suspicious intelligence with the enemy, whom he urges to lay aside the blinding prejudices of religious dogma and to join hands with him in the enforcement of peace. These plans Bohlmann describes with obvious acclaim, regretting the tragic refusal of Wallenstein's opponents to trust him. They were unable to see how one and the same man could show so much ruthlessness in his military expeditions and yet, after some time, express such deep concern for the well-being of the people. Wallenstein failed because his contemporaries were unable to understand the psychology of an extremely complex character and so were suspicious of it. Their realistic outlook stubbornly denied the possibility of a Saul turning into a Paul.

It is much easier to present Eugene of Savoy as a man who sincerely wished to build a unified and strong Reich stretching from Belgrade to Brussels, from Naples to the Baltic Sea. Eugene, who fought on all German frontiers, against the French in Italy, on the Rhine, and in the Netherlands, and against the Turks in the East, and who returned from his campaigns as the loyal servant of an emperor whom he yet surpassed on every important count, was first and last a soldier, as far as history knows. The novelist, however, can make him the silent or eloquent champion of a great political plan that prompted all his far-spread movements and fitted them into a Pan-Germanic dream.

For a combination of the adventurous with the political no better subject could be found than this little prince who, slighted by his master Louis XIV, *le Roi-Soleil*, escaped from France in the garb of a *petit abbé*, to transform his hurt pride into deadly hatred. His subsequent rise from Adjutant to the Duke Karl von Lothringen to Imperial Marshal provides all the incidents of a gripping story, except those of passion and love. Upon them is built the philosophical-political superstructure, the far-sighted, nation-building design with which the novelists now credit Eugene. There are easy ways and means of slipping such thoughts into the mind of the victim. They can be introduced either as the result of a sudden resolution made by the prince in the wrath of his youthful experience, a quick reply to the insult inflicted on him, or as a plan which, beginning as a practical military consideration, a working hypothesis for his many campaigns, gradually revealed itself to him, if not to others, as the blueprint of a future Germany, and with which he finally identified himself.

Ludwig Mathar (*Der Reichsfeldmarschall*) prefers the early conversion in the flight from France. He places it at the moment when the fugitive crosses his Rubicon, the Rhine; Eugene spots the spires of Strassburg, and his decision is made. This minster was once free, until Louis stole it from the Reich. And with clenched fists Eugene admonishes himself: Draw your sword, Eugene of Savoy, Duke of the Empire, Marshal of the Emperor, for its liberation. It would be interesting to question the author on the meaning of liberation, in this connexion. But Mathar rushes on, to make the conversion complete. Eugene's eyes look farther into the distance, to still another tower, that of St. Stephen in Vienna. There he sees wild hordes rushing forward from the East, on horseback and on foot—the Turks, incited to their predatory expedition by Louis XIV of France.

Walter von Molo[1] is much too experienced a writer to start Eugene on his career with a full-grown political vision; the very sub-title of his novel, "The Secret Emperor," indicates a much subtler approach. There are no trumpets here announcing the grandiose scheme of saving the German nation; instead, we are given a series of quietly executed deeds that insinuate rather than proclaim that Eugene more than the crowned head of the Empire is shaping its destiny. Eugene crosses the Rhine with the

[1]*Eugenio von Savoy* (Hamburg, n.d.).

[107]

understandable object of striking back at the one who had so deeply wronged him. His best chance to do so lies in joining the army of the enemies of France. This is, in the light of modern psychology, a very probable course of feeling and acting, though von Molo does not venture to suggest that the violent reaction represents merely a primitive outburst, for which a lofty motivation was found only afterwards, by way of rationalization. It is obvious that Eugene is fit material for a psychological novel, and that the Freudians, or at any rate the disciples of Adler, have missed a great opportunity in not taking advantage of the case of this slight, inconspicuous prince who out of spite and in order to compensate himself for his thwarted ambition became one of the greatest of field commanders.

In keeping with a method that selects and illumines only historically documented and decisive incidents, Mirko Jelusich (*Der Traum vom Reich*) evades the problem of when and how the conversion took place. Instead, he takes up the thread after the death of Emperor Leopold, with the inauguration of his successor Joseph and the summoning of Eugene, after the fall of Mirandola. It is only gradually that the dream of a greater Germany assumes more distinct outlines, and the technique of the author makes it clear enough that it is his own vision which is being spirited into the mind of Eugene. While the careful selection of incidents, from all over the historical scene of action, maintains the illusion of a faithful, realistic presentation of events, his subjective interspersions, on the other hand, permit the author to say all he wants to say and to reveal the intention of his own generation with the highest measure of precision. Eugene is made the perfect mouthpiece of modern *Grossdeutschland* and its promoters, whose programme he embodies with only minor adjustments. The *Drang nach dem Osten* here has its assigned place, though the Eastern enemies happen to be the Turks and Hungarians instead of the Russians. The Catholic Church in both its territorial and its spiritual ambitions comes in for a strong rebuff. Sweden is relegated to a very minor role in the far North, with a contemptuous frown at her neutrality. That France should appear in the garb of a European villain, the greatest menace to the German Reich, goes without saying. But even England is made the target of attacks, on the occasion of the ill-advised expedition against Toulon which, according to Jelusich, was undertaken at the request of an English admiral. It must, however, be admitted that all the novelists mentioned speak with respect of Marlborough, even if they consider Eugene a greater military genius. The recall of Marlborough by the Tories is treated as a calamitous incident, the result of what the German authors regard as the unworkable democratic two-party system. The historian Walter Elze[1] goes much further, using Eugene as a pretext to elaborate on the inveterate meanness of England. In 1712, England committed an act of treason by which the history of Europe and the fate of the world were changed. Prince Eugene embodied all the moral values to which England pays lip-service. On the eve of the final decision on the battle-field, England betrayed her mission, which was to establish a new order in Europe and in the whole world; and he quotes from Winston Churchill: "Nothing in the history of civilized nations surpasses this black treason." The novels generally show much less acerbity and a much greater sense of justice; if Eugene failed to realize what they consider to have been his dream of a unified Germany, he did so for many reasons. Among these the fall of Marlborough from governmental favour was a constituent factor, but by no means the only one, or the strongest.

Jelusich has a domestic as well as a foreign policy for his protagonist: the reduction of all internal opposition to impotence; the relegation of the ruling princes to the position of mere administrators; the division of the Reich not according to dynastic likes and dislikes but to agree with racial or tribal boundaries; the abolition of all internal customs barriers; the imposition of a uniform monetary system; and, most important of all, the infusion into all subjects of a national pride and of the feeling of

[1]*Der Prinz Eugen,* 1940. Other recent books of a more or less scholarly character are: Hellmuth Rössler, *Der Soldat des Reiches Prinz Eugen* (1934); Alfons von Czibulka, *Prinz Eugen* (1936); Viktor Bibl, *Prinz Eugen* (1941).

a common responsibility. Mention is, of course, also made of Eugene's plans for the colonization of the land along the Danube with German settlers. He describes this land to the Emperor: "There is black, rich soil, capable of giving bread to millions of people. True enough, this land is in the hands of the Turks, but they do not know what to do with it and have therefore forfeited all rightful ownership. It is your right to seize it because you know better than they what to do with it." To top it all, Eugene has ready in his pocket the military plan by which he will fan out into these fertile plains and take possession of them.

Jelusich's book at this juncture becomes a political document, not of Prince Eugene's day, but of our own, and not of the German mentality alone, but of imperialism in general. All the instincts and arguments of the expansionist are there: might is right; the people standing in the path of your ambition are of an inferior race; as such they have no claim to the bread-basket which your own superior people covet; the elimination of inferior tribes, far from being a crime, becomes a sacred duty. With shocking frankness, lust for power shows its hand in "The Dream of the Empire," making it, like all such dreams, regardless of where they originate, a nightmarish experience.

One would normally assume that from Prince Eugene the line of architects or at least prophets of the Third Reich would run to Frederick II of Prussia, and from him to Bismarck. Though the latter is frequently referred to in novels dealing with German life in the second half of the last century, there does not seem to be any evidence of a recent novel about him. The fate of Frederick is even more surprising for, with the exception of one very bulky novel, *Der grosse König* by Hans Heyck, an overstuffed biography, the German book market seems to have been deprived of this popular fare. Was it because the theme had been overdone, with nauseating monotony, by writers and movie producers? A number of booklets containing anecdotes, thoughts, or letters of Frederick and published during the recent war in inexpensive pocket editions (obviously intended as intellectual hard tack) damp our optimism.

In general the expert writer of historical fiction will prefer fields in which the documentary evidence compiled by the trained historian does not crowd out the novelist but rather leaves full scope for literary treatment and in fact needs the enlivening touch of imagination. How ordinary people lived at some period in the past, and how they were affected by towering historical figures or by the events precipitated by them, these things we would sooner learn from a good novelist than from the historian. Economic history is as good an example as any of a field which invites a division of labour between historian and novelist. For instance, to understand fully the economic set-up of some past time we have to be taken into the company of the common people, and here is a wonderful opportunity for a writer to use his imagination purposefully, in the elucidation of the habits, thoughts, and actions of a multitude of individuals whose activities only in the aggregate assume significance for the historian.

Medieval days, though not the most promising field for a clear-cut demarcation between historiography and fiction, will always remain a temptation for the imaginative writer as distinct from the historian proper. Hence, we surmise, the fact that never for long are we without a novel that hopes to be the successor to Scheffel's *Ekkehard* and to equal its still continuing popularity. Berchtold Gierer's *Geschlechter am See* seems to have come closest to realizing the great ambition, if the fact that the book received the reward of the German Municipal Corporation is any indication of its popularity. The author attempts to revive life in the fifteenth century, in the very corner of Germany which Scheffel selected for his novel and which can be rightly considered the cradle of German civilization, the districts surrounding Lake Constance. In tone the book differs from Scheffel's gay pageant of courtly ladies, decorous nuns, and urbane monks, for Gierer writes from the point of view of the suppressed peasants and the restricted artisans of the cities, whose struggle for freedom he supports. Hans Leip, in his novel *Das Muschelhorn*, takes us to the North, to illustrate the same social process in its reverberations among the farmers of Frisia and the townspeople of Hamburg. The most vibrant and most subtle record of the late Middle Ages is contained in Erika Mitterer's *Der Fürst der Welt,* which, for its psychological analysis of suppressed desires throbbing behind the walls of nunneries and for its description of the hopeless, inarticulate opposition of simple townsfolk to a state-inspired superstition and religious persecution, must rank as a masterpiece; here is a fine example of how the novelist can find a convincing explanation for much that the historian can only put down as strange and inexplicable fact. More will have to be said of these three grim pictures of an earlier time in chapter IX.

The incipient stage of capitalism in the fourteenth and fifteenth centuries has only recently captured the attention of fiction-writers. This discovery amounts to a literary event of prime importance. If, as we must presume, the historians had to do their spade-work first before the novelists could move in, it is equally obvious that without the supplementary creative imagination of some writers we should never have realized the many tints of this sociological and economic material, or its exciting parallels to modern life. The needful co-operation between novelist and historian, their mutual interdependence, are ably acknowledged and demonstrated in a monumental account of this period. *Der junge Herr Alexius,* by Otto Rombach, sets a standard for the combination of creative imagination and historical accuracy and documentation. The author frankly admits that his work owes its existence to the historical research of others, notably to the discovery of a bundle of letters in the Salem convent by the archivist Karl Obser. These letters, on closer investigation, were found to contain a mine of information on the Ravensburg Trading Company, one of the great corporations of merchants of the fifteenth and sixteenth centuries, with branches in Italy, France, Spain, Holland, and England. Sir Alexius Hilleson, one of the governors of this company, is moved into the centre of the novel. Interesting as his rise to great power is, Rombach must have felt that he owed it to the material placed at his disposal to record the life of the firm in its organic unity. The result is a truly historical novel, one in which we are carried away into a reality not easily apprehensible otherwise. It is very likely that a business man might find the book even more to his taste than a reader who is a layman in regard to the transactions of high finance—an indication of the measure to which Rombach succeeded in organizing his information into something living. We follow his story with much the same interest that a shareholder in the company must have felt; we are concerned as he must have been over all the problems involved: the relations of the firm, almost a synonym for the economic and social life of Ravensburg, with other such trading companies and with the various governments; the question of dropping certain articles from the list and looking out for new ones; the task of appointing the right kind of managers to the widely scattered branches; the attempt to edge into foreign markets; the means of transportation, across the Alps and over the oceans; the methods of keeping books and conducting business; and finally the question whether or not the company should try to get a foothold on the newly discovered continent of America. All these issues help to create the impression that an old era with its very special concerns has been recaptured. There are long chapters where we feel that we could do without the personal adventures of Alexius, so interesting is the picture of life in general; in other parts, however, the personal element has a significance all its own, notably where Alexius is concerned with his inner life, while promoting the financial interests of himself and of the company. His absorption of the artistic culture of Italy, France, and Holland serves as a strong reminder of the important role which business men played in propagating learning, in supporting artists, and in working toward international tolerance. The period Rombach describes knew nothing of the sickly belief in the incompatibility of active participation in life with serious cultural propensities; on the contrary, the two spheres seemed to thrive best when joined together.

A three-volume edition of documents concerning the Ravens-burg Trading Company which was compiled by Aloys Schulte[1] will give it a place in the consciousness of Germans equal to that held by the Welser and Fugger firms. The history of the latter two companies has for years received its adequate share of scholarly attention. That novelists were so slow in making use of the material is surprising; there seems to be no other reason for this neglect than the general disregard, among literary men, of economic matters.

The difference between Rombach's story and the Fugger novels by Eugen Ortner (*Glück und Macht der Fugger*; *Das Weltreich der Fugger*) is that between two types of historical novel. Rombach rewrote the dealings of the Ravensburg firm as they affected all those who were drawn into them, the governors and the draymen, the shareholders and the foreign agents. Ortner focuses attention on a few outstanding personalities, mainly on Jakob Fugger the Rich. In choosing to write the history of a personality rather than that of a collective organism he missed a great opportunity to advance the technique of historical fiction.

It is a far cry from the Ravensburg merchants with their ever alert sense of social responsibility towards all their employees and towards the whole town, whose prosperity depended on the company, to the group of financiers selling Panama Canal shares, in the eighties of the last century. For a novelist versed in the art of turning his camera rapidly to a variety of scenes and social layers, there could be no more interesting array of events than those connected with or leading up to the Panama scandal. Again the novelist is in small danger of trespassing on the preserves of the historian. For the latter the Panama scandal is largely a matter of financial and political entanglements; the novelist, on the other hand, will interpret cold figures in terms of the rising and falling hopes of millions of people, or in terms of bribery and fierce competition among the bankers of that time, in France and in the United States. Christoph Erik Ganter (*Panama*) has

[1]*Geschichte der grossen Ravensburger Handelsgesellschaft 1380-1530*, 3 vols. (1923).

[114]

done this and many other things that the gigantic project and the equally gigantic swindle would suggest to an imaginative mind. The contrast between the men who became rich by raising the funds, and the engineers and workers who performed the great feat of digging the canal, who struggled with a hostile territory and perished in large numbers, is well described and soberly reported. Moreover, Ganter knows the history of this vast project in all its ramifications, from both the technical and the financial angle; he is thus able to prepare the climax of the successful canalization in a dramatic fashion that takes us over the whole ground. Alexander von Humboldt begins the discussion of the possibility of connecting the two oceans; Louis Napoleon is seen to catch fire even in the days of exile; ere long the whole of France is agog with plans and speculations. There was no need for the author to trail along, as he does, the plot of a love story, since the collective effort fully suffices to sustain the reader's interest.

It appears that between January and July, 1943, Ganter's book was twice reissued, to a total of 93,000 copies—a success that may not be wholly due to the intrinsic merits of the story. Other reasons for its popularity are not far to seek: the pitiful roles of gullible victim or sharp promoter assigned to a number of French members of parliament must have won the applause of a reading public steeped in anti-democratic propaganda, as must have also the contention of the author that no less a statesman than Clemenceau was playing a dubious part in the Panama affair. More than a casual hint is dropped about the eager participation of Jewish bankers, though Ganter does not minimize the extent to which Christians were involved. For good patriotic measure he works into the story a garrulous but quietly heroic German doctor who, with his daughter, does much to relieve the plight of workers ailing and dying from malaria. As a matter of fact the doctor is credited with having made possible the continuation of the operations, through his method of exterminating the deadly flies. "The world today knows that it was not the skill of the engineers but the effects of coal oil, asphalt oil, and carbolic acid that led to the completion of the canal . . . the solution was allowed to work for twenty-four hours, whereupon it was ignited (as a thin layer covering the stagnant waters) and the procedure repeated. The result was that after February 20, 1906, no new cases of yellow fever in the canal zone were reported; malaria had all but disappeared and the isthmus, once the curse of the earth, a pest-hole, became and remained one of the healthiest tropical countries." History may or may not bear out the author on this point; he writes, at any rate, quite factually about it. His book ends on a note of deep concern lest the great accomplishment be endangered by threats of a world war. The opening of the canal coincided with the day on which the shots of Sarajevo were fired. Here for once a German author is genuinely perturbed lest the concerted efforts of thousands of brave men be wiped out by the demon of war.

For many, novels such as Rombach's and Ganter's provide a pleasant means of acquiring information about past times. That there is a very wide demand for literature which imparts knowledge in this form is evinced by the popularity of the novels of Rudolf Brunngraber (*Opiumkrieg*; *Zucker aus Cuba*), works that have had unusually large sales, in spite of their author's slight talent for interlacing history with fiction or doing justice to the economic and political significance of such events as the development of cane sugar planting in Cuba, or the definite efforts of the English to enforce their opium trade on China in the middle of the last century.

The impact of technical and natural sciences upon the life of nations is one of the factors which modern historians feel obliged to analyse more fully than did their predecessors, who were inclined to narrow the concept of historically relevant material to political and military events, and who took cognizance of other influences only in cases where these compelled worldwide attention, as did for instance geographical discoveries, religious movements, and social upheavals. Literature has kept pace with this trend; indeed the novelists have perhaps been marching a few steps ahead of the historians.

When the inventor or discoverer belongs to our own time, we experience the added fascination of seeing recent events in their transition into history. We who happen to be alive today have witnessed the appearance of at least three inventions which more than any other scientific or technical innovations have aroused our wonder: the automobile, the aeroplane, and the film. The omission of radio, in this connexion, is justified when we consider that its effect on our imaginative faculties has been much slighter. Any novelist working close to those who first experimented with one of these three inventions can count on our quickened attention, just as an early Ford model proves an irresistible attraction to the curious spectator.

Guido Bagier in *Das tönende Licht* has apparently been the first German novelist to attempt to deal with the beginnings of movie projecting and sound recording. As one would expect of an author who treats of highly technical things and their history, a mass of source-material was consulted; that the author's imagination, with all the information gathered from German, French, English, and American sources, was still able to flow in the channels of epic fiction, is much to his credit. Though Edison and his collaborator Krüsi are rightly pictured as the leading men in the field of early cinematography, others like Lumière, Decaux, the Pathés, Carpentier, Moisson, Continsouza, Rabilloud, Henry Joly receive their due share of praise. As a matter of fact one of the revelations the readers of Bagier's book will receive is that of the immense collective effort, during and before the days of Edison, that was necessary to achieve a successful product, the prototype of present-day movie projectors. The author, though possessing only a fair command of style, excels in his understanding of the whole background out of which a technical product originates. For many other factors besides those of a purely scientific character contribute to give it a useful shape. Financial backing must be obtained; the proper social attitude is a part of the pattern. For instance, as long as moving pictures were meant to be a cheap form of entertainment for county fairs and vaudeville shows, the inventive genius was kept off the right track.

When a higher cultural-social aim was envisaged, construction improved.

Some Germans, especially Steinmetz, also played an honourable part in the perfection of movie equipment. Bagier brings this to our attention without depreciating the much greater contribution made by others. Not the least important lesson his novel drives home is the necessity for international co-operation, if there is to be full utilization of the stores of ideas and of material resources that are scattered all over the world.

The early days of flying by aeroplane might well attract the novelist. Bits of information about these days appear sporadically in novels dealing with the beginning of our century and tend to whet our appetite for a more comprehensive treatment. If German writers so far have been loath to re-enact the thrills of the first man travelling through the air, this is most likely due to the fact that the Germans, prominent though they were in working out the theory of flying, had to watch from the ground the spectacular sight of the machines actually lifting into the air. It is all the more to be appreciated that it was a German who recently undertook to revive the memory of a half-forgotten flying pioneer, Geo Chavez, who was the first to fly over the Simplon mountain range (September, 1910). For some reason Rudolf Timmermanns chose to write his story (*Aufzeichnungen, Flug und Tod des Geo Chavez*) in the form of a fictitious diary kept by Chavez; this and the emphasis that is put on an emotional interlude with a young woman are chiefly responsible for the scarcity of more technical details which, after all, are what make the beginnings of aviation so interesting. In this respect a novel by Hans Rabl (*Das Ziel in den Wolken*, 1937) keeps much closer to the facts of early aviation. Rabl writes of the first, highly secretive doings on a Berlin aerodrome. He is not quite free from a grudge against the foreigners who had such a clear advantage over the German birdmen, but he does not withhold credit where credit is due, particularly in the case of Orville Wright and the men he brought to Germany to manufacture and demonstrate his type of aeroplane. Rabl at once gets busy, however, finding a promising rival among his countrymen. The ambition of a young German flier and a love story, simple enough to invent for a period when no respectable father would allow his daughter to fall in love with a flier, make up the novel. Yet for all that it remains historical fiction. To be sure, there are no definitely identifiable historical events or characters except for a few such as Orville Wright and the German Hans Grade. The historical patina is given more clearly by the material paraphernalia, for instance, the type of plane these men were flying, or the awe-inspiring costumes they wore. Moreover, by reminding the reader of his own reminiscences of those distant days when he saw the first aeroplane or when he entered for the first time the strangely exciting atmosphere of a flying field, Rabl's novel stimulates a kind of personal historical contemplation.

We have yet to see a novel in which the now historical days of the first automobile receive more than a casual reference. The time will soon be here when young and even middle-aged authors will no longer be able to speak with first-hand knowledge of those days, but will have to depend on imagination or historical records. One source to which they will have to turn is Eugen Diesel's masterly presentation (*Autoreise 1905*) of the atmosphere of the early *Herrenfahrer* and his family, soon after the start of the century. In dedicating his reminiscences to his children, the author speaks of an innocent little book which but for the fact that everything described in it has actually occurred, might seem a piece of imaginative fiction. Future generations, and the book deserves to survive for a long time to come, will be grateful both for its historical accuracy and for its literary qualities. Diesel has the taste of an artist in making a careful selection from what must have been a welter of material. First comes the acquisition of the car, quite an elaborate process in those days. Then the family start out on their first overland trip, with father and the chauffeur taking turns at the wheel, while mother puts up as best she can with this new type of locomotion and pretends to be enthused in spite of much discomfort. The journey entails, of course, its round of technical and other incidents, though these are by no means the only experiences remembered. Young Diesel has his eyes wide open; more important than that, the author adds to actual memories thoughts and conclusions that must have come to him later in life. On some occasions his so-called report assumes the proportions of a gloomy prophecy of the future of Germany. Among other things he warns his countrymen not to consider themselves the sole guardians of the Germanic tradition. Especially, observations made in Switzerland (though at some later date, we presume) challenge him to insert some strict censoring of German anti-democratic feelings. "Under the surface varnish [of Swiss life], put on in thick layers during the nineteenth century, there was much of which the Germans knew nothing, something thoroughly Germanic in the sense of a tradition centuries old. . . . There prevailed a great quality of taste in a highly developed though sober culture, unusually reliable working standards. . . . A slice of the old German substance has survived in Switzerland, though to be sure a large portion of continuously regenerating German substance has not become as fully integrated in Switzerland as it has in Germany."

Diesel is aware of the rapidity with which Continental material surroundings, inventions, dress and manners move from the present into the past, a peculiarly European phenomenon, as he sees it. With increasing swiftness Europeans are acquiring the faculty of seeing even the present as something quaint that will soon become out-moded, old-fashioned, and historical. They produce history faster than primitives or other, non-European peoples do. It goes without saying that literature is heavily involved in this process, passively by resignedly accepting the transformation of contemporaneity into history, and actively by accelerating the regression of the present into the past and helping the historical patina to grow.

This is exactly what some German writers have been doing. We have already noted references in recent fiction to the assassination of Archduke Franz Ferdinand and his wife in 1914. The event, taken by historians to be the spark that brought about a world conflagration, has come to be treated by novelists as the watershed dividing an older period from the modern one. To many of them all that has happened since is in some sense current history, and for that reason history of a kind with which we cannot deal objectively. Our personal fortunes, opinions, and passions are involved in it to an extent that does not permit a detached, epic presentation. Novels on life after Sarajevo are written in the first person, figuratively speaking, by partisans of one or the other creed. The period before Sarajevo, on the other hand, is made to look more and more historical; its once heatedly discussed issues the novelists now present *sine ira et studio*. The aura around formerly sacrosanct institutions and persons, such as the Hohenzollern dynasts, is now altered by irony or boredom; serenity rather than tense watchfulness marks the approach to those days whose manners, ideas, and methods today evoke a feeling of quaint remoteness. The dividing line which a generation ago ran through 1848, or perhaps through 1871, has been advanced to run through 1914.

There is an understandable fascination for novelists in treading on ground which is in the process of becoming historical. To some it still looks green; vestiges of life are yet abundant. For middle-aged authors there is the additional attraction of their youth having been spent in that period, and with it withering away into history. Still others take an obvious delight in exaggerating the remoteness of all that occurred before 1914.

The number of novels that transpose us into the period around 1900 is, of course, large. They do so without their authors in every case experiencing and conveying the impression of a slightly unusual situation. A few authors, however, seem to have chosen the period for the express purpose of enjoying its newly historical character.

Damals bei uns daheim, by Hans Fallada; *Langsam steigt die Flut*, by Hermann Stahl; *Eine Schicksalssymphonie*, by Friedrich Schreyvogel are all works of the chronicle type; they all mirror life at the turn of the century, but each approaches it from a distinctly different point of view. Schreyvogel is at home in the Austrian scene, especially in Vienna; Stahl covers the Rhineland;

Fallada's centre is first in Berlin and then shifts to Leipzig. *Damals bei uns daheim* is the most obviously autobiographical, a report of the author's youth up to the time of his adolescence. The shots of Sarajevo do not echo in it, but we expect to hear them almost any moment in the last chapter. Though using the first person Fallada takes the liberty of digressing into descriptions of general conditions wherever the personal experiences invite these more objective complements. An account of life in the family of a higher civil servant, the book neatly embalms the *mores* of their time, their social conventions, holidaying, schooling, and *Wandervogel* activities. If these are manifestations of life that merely change without becoming better or worse, the author also touches upon issues of a more critical nature. Most interesting in this respect is the portrait of his father, a judge of sterling qualities, conscientious, hard-working, but lacking the courage to say all he knows and thinks. He is very sceptical about the legal practice and the civil courts of his time, but buries his misgivings in piles of documents and silences his conscience with the satisfaction of being a faithful servant of the state. He is an example of the tragic neutralization of the sense of social responsibility among so many men of good education and (within limits) irreproachable character.

The will to react against undesirable situations, so signally absent in Fallada's story, stirs vigorously, if only sporadically, in *Eine Schicksalssymphonie*. In this "symphony" figures Kress, an engineer and early prophet of the flying age whose friends try hard to win official recognition for him as the man who first in human history lifted a heavier-than-air machine from the ground, if only for a few seconds. There is, too, a patriarchal manufacturer of furniture who refuses to read the handwriting on the wall which spells the doom of small business, and who has to be told by his son that while one may have a high respect for an out-and-out capitalist, or for a real revolutionary, a half-hearted capitalist who is afraid of both will fast become a ridiculous figure. In each of these cases a losing battle is being waged. Blériot comes to Vienna to receive a tumultuous ovation, with Kress among the spectators; the latter is magnanimous enough to rejoice over the fact that his prophecies have come true, even if his own theoretical and practical contributions are overshadowed and outdroned by the daring young Frenchman. As for the small manufacturer, the reader foresees his defeat without the author expressly confirming it. The substance of Schreyvogel's book is, however, not concerned with controversial issues, but is of a panoramic character, reflecting life in the Austrian capital in the days when Eleonora Duse enraptured her audience, and Brahms treated a circle of friends to musical revelations. The painter Hans Makart is shown at the height of his ephemeral reputation; Lueger, the mayor of Vienna, and Billroth, famous as surgeon and pianist, appear in sharply delineated episodes. Then, a sudden shock to all but the few whose hobby was politics, the war clouds darken the scene. If the author is as well informed about the general aspects of the period as he is in regard to details, we must accept his view that the war took Vienna, and in fact the whole of Austria, by surprise. People by and large were too much absorbed in making a living, or in making life worth while, or quite often in both, to expect anything else of their government but the greatest anxiety to preserve peace. When war broke out, the cultural tradition was strong enough, after the first stupor cleared away, to reassert itself and to proclaim its will to survive, come what might. Thus, while we see the plunge of a nation into the turmoil of war, we also seem to know that its inner life is such that it will rise again, sooner or later. Somehow Austrian civilization must have developed cultural values with such a strong primacy over all others that here the process of history undergoes a significant variation: its political and social institutions seem to be more susceptible to the corrosion of time than its cultural activities. This fact may be related to the musical texture of Austrian culture, and to the greater resilience of music amid political, economic, and social tremours. In this light the title of Schreyvogel's book would seem to be very appropriate, pointing as it does to the symphonic continuity of Austrian life, which will outlast drastic changes that in other countries would disrupt all traditions, cultural as well as social.

Fallada makes no claim in his book that anything in his

youthful environment was worth saving or strong enough to survive the holocaust of the war, once it came. The upper middle classes he grew up with were good in many ways, respectable, cultured, devoted, and ambitious without becoming nakedly selfish. If they last another fifty or a hundred years, very well; if they should disappear tomorrow, something new will move into their position and serve the purpose just as well. Hermann Stahl's vast panorama of German life between the Franco-Prussian War and 1914, *Langsam steigt die Flut,* likewise evokes no more than a passing regret at the end for the impending doom. The few things in the panorama that we come to value, such as a plucky young middle-class girl, or a resourceful youth who over-comes a more than ordinary measure of hardship without losing his warm-heartedness or his sense of humour, are, so we assume, of the very essence of life and will emerge again, no matter what conditions prevail after the war. The rest, if we except the amenities of small-town life and of folk-lore in the Rhineland, are not worth being taken into a modern Noah's Ark; they are, in fact, in many instances contributing factors to the rising flood to which the title of the novel makes allusion. For this flood is fed both from within the country and from outside it. The en-circlement of Germany, by England, France, and Russia, will account for the final catastrophe, but internal weakness also invites the disaster. In the government the author depicts a vacillating leadership, given to bombast and with no sense of the realities of European life. Throughout the length and breadth of the country goes on a mad scramble for financial and social advantages, accompanied by disunity between employer and worker, envy of neighbours, and, worst of all, a widespread feel-ing of boredom engendered by a spiritual vacuum.

What makes the novel this almost exhaustive chronicle of the period in question is a deftly ramified action. Each of three young orphans is turned over to a different foster home: the girl goes to a gentle old spinster entombed in the Biedermeier tradition; one of her brothers, seemingly the luckiest, is given the dubious advantage of a well-to-do city home in Cologne and will in time become a spoiled brat and unscrupulous law student; his younger brother has by far the hardest lot to endure, as he is presented to a typical *bourgeois* in a small town. While events centre around this third child whom we see grow up and, in his growth, reflect the period, the author never loses sight of his brother and sister and thus has opportunity to adjust his search-light to different social levels. His knowledge is quite equal to such a diversified task, and so is his range of emotions. Tragic and comic incidents, satire and criticism all have their turn without distorting the fundamental mood of historical detachment. If it were not for an occasional expression of warm sympathy or spontaneous disgust we should be ready to believe that Stahl writes of a very remote past.

The individual temperaments of Fallada, Stahl, and Schreyvogel, and their predominantly artistic intentions, have no doubt much to do with their readiness to relegate the time of their own youth to history. Against this it is well to remember that individuals and nations all have their touchy spots, their historical memories that can easily be fanned into reviving passions. Most Germans, in the nineteenth and twentieth centuries, felt very definite reactions whenever the word "France" was mentioned. Indeed it is doubtful whether any other word produced as quick and definite a reaction of hostility. To say that the word "Rhine" runs a close second is largely a tautology. The popularity of Eugene of Savoy as a hero in German fiction stems mainly from his anti-French bias. Authors who wish to capitalize on such a bias have, however, no difficulty in finding much better fuel for the flames of resentment against or hatred of the French. If the Napoleonic Wars are felt to be too remote to arouse very violent passions any longer (the Franco-Prussian War, ending with a complete German triumph, could only serve the ends of literary sadism), the French encroachment upon German territory after 1918 provides excellent propagandistic material. The difficulties of Germans in Alsace-Lorraine after the Armistice, the occupation of the Rhineland, and the march into the Ruhr district are so many memories that touch off violent emotions. Diesel's observation on the rapid historicizing of modern life must be corrected in the light of such danger spots which can cause explosions on very slight provocation.

Alsace-Lorraine is of particular significance as a scene of German novels. It is a country saturated with history, and one not easily surpassed in mellow natural beauty and cultural richness; yet its greatest lure, for one who is interested in human relationships, derives from a social structure which is singularly diversified, for instance by lingering sympathies with the former régimes, French or German as the case may be, and by marriages between Latins and Germans, the children of these unions being often driven apart and set one against another in times of war. The very air of Alsace-Lorraine seems to be filled with tension, and yet it is also filled with *joie de vivre,* songs, and festive moods. Were it not for the fact that the people speak two different languages or a mixture of the two unsuited for higher literary purposes, one could not think of a more fertile milieu for a novelist to work in.

Undaunted by linguistic difficulties two Germans have recently ventured to give a vast literary account of life in Alsace-Lorraine, in one case before, and in the other even after, the First World War. By allowing relatively few French interspersions and by bringing the native Alamannic dialect, wherever it had to be used, close to literary German, both E. M. Mungenast (*Der Zauberer Muzot*) and Hans Holzach (*Der goldene Rahmen*) have avoided the danger of leaving their thoughts and feelings at the mercy of a very limited vernacular. This, and the comprehensiveness of their epic pictures, are all the two authors have in common. In their social and political attitudes they stand at opposite poles. Holzach, tolerant of the French and interested in them because they are different and therefore stimulating, alludes to a possible conflict not between the two races but between the workers and the middle classes. He devotes more space to the easy-going existence of the latter, to their ceremonious society and to their general penchant for good living, perhaps from a melancholy sympathy with a way of life that has reached its zenith and is now on the descent.

Mungenast's Alsatian novel, running to more than 800 pages (almost twice as long as *Der goldene Rahmen*), hardly misses an important political event or a public character of note in the history of the province between 1870 and 1918. Likewise, in the large number of fictitious characters there is a variety such as the German novel has not brought into existence since Jakob Wassermann, with this difference that Mungenast's men, women, and children originate in the realities of a circumscribed area. The branches growing on the trunk of the main plot are accordingly numerous. Legitimate and illicit love, murder and tender lyricism, art and religion, business and politics all come together here. Yet with all that we are ever reminded that the author, in the final analysis, is developing a political thesis, the gist of which is the incompatibility of the two races, French and German, and hence the necessity for one or the other to rule the country with a strong hand. The failure of the Germans to understand this political axiom after the re-conquest in 1871 causes Mungenast to make very bitter strictures about the Prussian administration. However, when in 1918 the French move in their more drastic measures, such as the expulsion of the German element, are by no means as understandingly accepted as the logic of the thesis would demand. French inhumanity as exposed by Mungenast seems idyllic in the light of what has happened since, which should remind us that even a minor excess against basic human rights today will lead to a worse one tomorrow. Unlike Holzach, Mungenast makes no attempt to find a *modus vivendi* for French and Germans (or for any other nation and the Germans). "Muzot," one of the characters is heard to say, "we are Germans . . . no nation on earth understands a German . . . no other nation will ever be able to understand him and this, Muzot, is not his tragedy, but that of the others. . . . A German searches for God, the others search for idols. . . ." If some of these Germanophiles choose to stay in Alsace, it is not, of course, to fit into the new order, but to await and possibly prepare for the day of liberation. This is also the attitude of the principal character in *Zwischen den Mächten*, by Anna Maria Falkenstern, and Roland Betsch (*Ballade am Strom*) surveys the history of the last hundred years on the

Western boundary, from Napoleon to the separatist movement, quite obviously with the intention of preparing the stage for another attempt to cross the Rhine in force.

Mungenast speaks out of the bitterness of a vanquished aspiration, his book having been written before the Second World War. It is interesting to see that three books, most likely written after the defeat of France in 1940, show much more sympathy with the French, who are no longer considered incapable of understanding the Germans and of co-operating with them. Carl Rothe (*Olivia*) analyses the psychology of a young Rhenish girl who is in love with both a French officer of the occupation army and a blind German veteran of the First World War. Hans Werlberger (*Wolkentanz*) and Roland Krug von Nidda (*Französische Elegie*), with almost identical intentions, write of Frenchmen who, though they have friendly contacts with Germans, are yet unable to see the light and to advocate in their homeland co-operation with the Third Reich. It is when the heroes of both these novels fall prisoners to the Germans in 1940 that they admit their mistakes and pledge collaboration for the establishment of peace in Europe. The two books are a striking example of the fact that dealing with current political events does not necessarily mean dealing with history. These and many other novels of the years after 1918 are marked for complete disappearance. It will be some time before German novelists can rewrite the history of their people after 1918 with an objectivity and in a spirit that are acceptable to the Western world. Fallada, Stahl, and Schreyvogel were right when they set at 1914 the boundary line up to which the German historical novel may move.

In contrast to the eager preoccupation with political, military, and social history in German novels, the history of thought has been almost neglected. We have it, of course, on the authority of Goethe, and latterly of Thomas Mann, that great intellectual figures make poor material for fiction. It is, we are told, more advisable to choose the heroes of novels from among men of ordinary calibre. Either because this piece of advice was heeded or because it was confirmed by unsuccessful attempts, a good

German novel with Kant, Lessing, Goethe, Hölderlin, or Hegel as its central figure is yet to come. In *Lotte in Weimar,* however, Thomas Mann disregarded his own misgivings concerning fiction heroes of high intellectual qualities, and has shown that the difficulty, if it exists, can be overcome.

Paracelsus, living in remote times and expressing himself cryptically enough to permit of a subjective interpretation, has not tempted any marked reversal of this general avoidance in novels of outstanding thinkers and philosophers. Copernicus and Kepler, and Jakob Böhme have attracted a few novelists. Copernicus and Kepler both had to face a hostile world with what they knew to be a more reasonable view of the universe and of the motion of celestial bodies. They were regarded with great misgivings by Lutherans and Catholics alike, and Kepler was actually persecuted by both religious factions; for indeed even the reform movement developed quickly its own form of narrow-mindedness and superstition. The authors of five recent Copernicus and Kepler novels seem to be Protestants. As such they may be counted on to lash out against Catholic obscurantism. They deal equally sternly, however, with the Wittenberg lights who denounced Copernicus as a heretic, and with the South German Protestants who intrigued against Kepler. The reader is all but expressly cautioned to keep in mind that radical firebrands at all times put new life into the superstition and anti-intellectualism which they pretend to fight.

Fritz Mettenleiter (*Nikolaus Kopernikus*), Will-Erich Peuckert (*Nikolaus Kopernikus*), and Alfred Karrasch (*Kopernikus*) all point accusingly to the process of petrifaction which set in so soon in Protestantism. Karrasch speaks of a Luther whose challenges solidified into dogma and who became a pope in his own domain, intolerant towards all who could not completely agree with him. But none of them go any farther; instead, they commend Copernicus for the serene patience that bade him withdraw from the world and leave his work for posterity to judge. As this is what Copernicus actually did, his biographers are excused for not being bolder, just as they were protected in case their emphasis on acquiescence and on trust in the slow-grinding mills of God, or of truth, attracted official suspicion. For, needless to say, these novels could have been regarded as an encouragement to those who suffered from a similar disregard of some truth they were trying to expound.

It is different with Kepler. While Copernicus was complacent, the former was stubborn, a bold fighter, and since his most admirable bout was fought against the authority of secular powers more than against Protestant and Catholic clerics, the novelist is lured into dangerous territory. The incident referred to is the trial of Kepler's mother as a witch, when he saved her from torture and death only by great exertions which in turn endangered his own life and liberty.

Bertold Keppelmüller (*Das Gesetz der Sterne*) passes quietly over Kepler's hurrying home to attack the sacrosanct judicial institutions in order to save his mother. Was the author afraid of heroizing, as a true account necessarily would, the combination of rationality and courage which Kepler embodied in rare fashion? Yet in other respects Keppelmüller goes out of his way to show Kepler as a man who early in his life came to disdain the wisdom of the appointed secular and spiritual rulers, preferring instead to dwell in a higher sphere where harmony prevailed and calm science reigned. His progress in human dignity the author measures in terms of his detachment from ephemeral concerns and his serene contemplation of the world from high above. Nor does Keppelmüller fail to draw obvious conclusions from his observations, namely, that true human dignity is a rare achievement and almost incompatible with the behaviour of the masses, and that we are still far from a society that will value and practise the virtues of intellectual integrity and nobility of mind. All this is in strange contrast to the flatteries the people had served to them in the Third Reich.

Regrettable as it is that Keppelmüller failed to present Kepler the fearless fighter for reason and justice and for the application of scientific thought to social problems, we draw comfort from the fact that Olaf Saile (*Kepler*, 1938) enters with delight into the astounding details of the trial. He shows how Kepler punctured the evidence of church and state witnesses and scathingly exposed a superstition that linked any accidental misfortune of man or beast with the sinister machinations of witches, forcing in the end not only the release of his mother but also a revision of the regulations governing the hearing of witnesses. For Saile, Kepler the champion of human rights and of the application of clear thinking to all spheres of life is as venerable as Kepler the mathematician and astronomer who could hear above the din of worldly quarrels the harmony of a scientifically defined cosmic order.

The life of the mystic Jakob Böhme was, if anything, even less eventful than that of Copernicus. His enemies never quite succeeded in preferring a charge of heresy against him, and so he was left to work at his trade (shoemaking), to think and write, and to hold long conversations with his sympathizers, mostly of the landed nobility. Rather than pad the scant biographical material, Edith Mikeleitis, in her novel about Böhme, *Das ewige Bildnis*, relies on the inner world of the venerable sage, on his words, and especially on his ability to make his listeners see the material world as radiant with the emanation from an all-pervading divine love. Her emphasis is on Böhme's faculty to preserve his belief in a benign Divinity in spite of the reality of so much evil among men, rather indeed because of it; for it is the "resistance" of the world to eternal tranquillity that provokes men into action, good and bad action. "Resistance there must be, because a clear and silent will is like nothing and produces nothing . . . neither darkness nor light, neither life nor death." The author hastens to proclaim, through her mystic philosopher, that things eternal are not affected by the pains and evils of existence, but continue indestructibly beautiful. Here and in many similar passages Böhme speaks, of course, as a spectator who can do little to repair a world that to him seems out of joint, except comfort himself and others by practising a *sub specie aeternitatis* perspective. From every indication Edith Mikeleitis was attracted to Böhme by this approach and addresses herself to readers who will appreciate the safe refuge of hope in contemplation. The tragedy is that both the need of this remedy and the remedy itself betray a paralysing fear of taking good action. What is worse, anyone who crosses the faint line that divides mysticism from pseudo-religion may quote Böhme's words as the go-signal for action of the most ruthless kind, intended to help the divine plan by producing the necessary "resistance." Ricarda Huch, whom no one will accuse of cynicism, once made a similarly dangerous (because ambiguous) statement to the effect that sinning is an indispensable prerequisite for genuine religious experience (*Luthers Glaube,* 1916).

9 Fundamental Moods

THE official mood, under National Socialism, was one of sweeping optimism, a *Lebensanschauung* filled with the exuberance of being Nordic, of having the good fortune to live at a time when Germany had achieved her real stride and could look forward to unlimited expansion, physically and ideologically.

This boisterous faith in the national or biological health, and the undisputed acceptance of life as a force that has its own propagation as its main goal are painfully reflected in a type of literature which introduced a new subdivision in the field of pornography: sexual braggartism. Here the rational element has been reduced almost to vanishing-point.

The vulgarity of this naked will-to-propagate was such that no self-respecting author, no writer of wisdom in contact with cultural traditions could afford to be associated with it. A person with a sensitive mind understands that there is an interplay between instinct and reason, between irrational inspiration and controlled thought. What is more, he also knows that a crudely physical enjoyment of life leaves a number of more refined aspirations atrophied and vast spheres of complex but gratifying experiences untouched. In fairness to literary standards in Germany it must be pointed out that if sexual ruffianism was popular in some quarters, there were many readers who demanded a nobler interpretation of life, and appreciated works written to meet this demand.

E. M. Mungenast was, according to information available, well received by the critics and openly hailed as a trump card in recent German fiction. Yet from him has come a novel *Der Pedant oder die Mädchen in der Au* in which the harmonious blending of instinct with reason, of passion with decorum and self-control is given the most serious concern and presented with clarity and with a perfection that carries conviction. The *Mädchen* referred to, four of them, all of marriageable age and longing to find husbands, take risks, in spite of the conservative background provided by their widowed mother, which a generation ago would have been judged dangerous and unbecoming. The reference is, of course, not so much to their aquatic performances in the near-by river, as to the readiness with which they let emotion triumph over the restraint imposed by social convention. If all ends well for them, with a triple marriage and a budding romance for the youngest sister, it is not because they have been lucky where others have been deceived and jilted, but because with their naturalness the girls combine a deeply ingrained knowledge of true values and exercise a rational faculty that is an integral part of their personality. It is this unobtrusive intelligence that creates the beauty of a young generation trained to be free in manners, but not freed from them. The behaviour of the girls is constantly under the control of a valid form of tradition which ensures that society's interests as well as their own will be considered. The difference between stale and meaningful convention is brought out when a cousin, the pedant of the title, makes his appearance. He lets it be known that he is willing to marry one of the sisters. But being a pedant—not in the extreme sense of a caricature, but in that of a narrow-minded kill-joy— he frowns upon all naturalness, thus indicating his need for the very emancipation he so dislikes. As long as he is on the scene we feel that the girls are to a great extent right in their independent ways, even if such independence leads one of them to run after a chance acquaintance, a soldier, and to play hostess to him in a hotel room. But when things have gone so far, much too far in the opinion of the pedant, though not in the estimate of common sense, a checking influence is invariably set in motion, through the mother of the girls, who understands both human nature and the vital significance of good form and ethical principles. She has never expected blind obedience from her daughters, but she counts on their circumspection and intelligent kindness. It is her conviction that the girls will learn, not by coercion on her part, but in the course of insisting on a high standard of mental and, if possible, also physical excellence, and of being satisfied only with true love from intelligent, public-spirited men. These they find indeed, and do not pause to reflect on the fact that their chosen ones come from a socially inferior level.

The result of such a blending of decorum with warm feminine feeling is a mood of hopeful expectation, a readiness to believe that life can become a worth-while experience, provided that the promptings of nature remain in accord with the dictates of reason and with the urges of a kind heart. If Mungenast shares with the official bios-philosophers a keen delight in the vitality of youth, he also knows that physical health must be used to absorb knowledge and wisdom, and a sense of social responsibility, if men are to be made truly human. It is only when nature and culture meet, in one and the same person, or in a harmonious group of people, that life realizes its greatest possibilities.

Georg Rendl, another writer exhaling a mood of instinctive happiness, is equally convinced of the intrinsic value of existence, yet for different reasons. His novel *Ein fröhlicher Mensch* is expressly declared to be a book about the riches of life. These riches are not the humanistic foundations of Mungenast's philosophy, not the cultural accomplishments of his four girls and their mother, and even less their material possessions and delight in physical well-being. The serene man of Rendl's novel is, in the opening chapters, a young boy, the son of a hard-working mountain farmer, a ray of sunshine in rather drab surroundings; as he grows older he shows an almost miraculous aptitude for transforming his environment materially and spiritually, succeeding where others have failed. His gloomy parents come under the spell of his radiant confidence, and the villagers owe him a debt of gratitude for the presence of mind by which he averts a flood, and for the intelligence with which he talks a government official out of an attempt to collect taxes from the impoverished farmers. These and other deeds he performs with a magic, angelic touch of common sense and serenity. The secret

[135]

of his life lies, in the final analysis, less in his natural abilities and more in his spiritual strength; he believes in a benevolent God whose aim it is to release himself into the world, through the medium of Christian candour. This spiritual agency the reader feels to be something real, a force that will actually influence and transform the world. Far from working in a vacuum, or in a world of pre-established harmony, the spiritual force meets more often than not with strong resistance. The world around serene Engelbrecht is filled with the dangers that come from hostile nature and from selfish men. The reality of an originally cruel world is conquered only by dint of a hard struggle and by absolute reliance on the power of the soul to achieve what alone is worth achieving: the increasing material and spiritual happiness of the people around us.

Rendl's faith in life stems from his simple, sincere Christian convictions; his ultimate message is that Christian ethics and their serious application to society can still be relied upon to solve the world's pressing social and spiritual problems. If you have Christianity, and if you practise it, life will not deceive you. To be socially minded is the modern, and perhaps at the same time the oldest, manifestation of the Christian spirit. Possession of this spirit is not at all incompatible with a joyous participation in life, nor is gloominess an essential attribute of piety. If you think it is, so Engelbrecht tells his father, you might just as well wish that all flowers should turn grey and trees black, and that the birds instead of singing should weep.

Humanism and Christian faith appear in Mungenast and Rendl with the force of a mood of instinctive joy; its presence in Germany, during the Third Reich, is not surprising, even though its literary manifestation may be.

There are others who have lost their childhood faith in either religion or humanism; held in the thralls of gloom they struggle, with varying intensity, towards new hopes and new ethical or religious beliefs. That deep gloom should be the fundamental mood of quite a few German novels is not necessarily the result of the philosophical existentialism now inundating art and literature. General conditions can account fully for the origin of a deep-rooted anxiety in sensitive men.

The mood of gloom darkens almost every page in Erika Mitterer's voluminous novel *Der Fürst der Welt*. She discovers a world of despair, and its hopelessness is contagious. Like others to be mentioned who take the same gloomy attitude, she chooses a medieval background to illustrate the abysmal frustration which is at times the lot of mankind. Her broad panorama of pre-Reformation days in Germany reveals many commendable literary gifts such as a firm grip on plot; innumerable narrative ramifications are carefully planned, and a vast amount of historical knowledge is unobtrusively woven into the design of the novel. Yet this design is emotionally conceived and the lasting impression of her work is that of a predominantly melancholy apprehension of life. Human beings for this female Schopenhauer are synonymous with outcasts. Here we see knights for whom life consists of an endless row of drab days interspersed with acts of violence and injustice, teachers who are lacking in all refinement, farmers smarting under the yoke of an economic system in which changes are long overdue, towns where the poor become poorer every day and the well-to-do live in perpetual fear of envious neighbours and greedy monks. All these groups are entangled in unending quarrels with one another. Worst of all, those who ought to know something about the good life are more exposed to temptation and yield to it more readily than simple laymen: pious father superiors become involved in love affairs and crimes; nuns yearning for mystic union with God fall into the hands of hypocritical seducers, to end their days at the stake. There is hardly a person of any account who does not come to grief in some form or other; the few who manage to survive are quite often the last ones to whom we should like to entrust the perpetuation of the human race or the improvement of civilization: vagabonds, wretches living in the deep forests, or proletarians whom no worldly or spiritual power attempts to rescue from their abject misery.

This, be it noted, is not the etching of a corrosive satirist.

[137]

On the contrary, it is with a bleeding heart that Erika Mitterer records these conditions, which are contrary to her fervent hopes. True enough, a few humanist scholars succeed in dodging the blood-thirsty dragons of obscurantism and superstition and manage to eke out a precarious existence between the warring factions. But the majority of people, especially the women, have nothing to look forward to. Their one hope for a fuller and more peaceful life, religion, invariably fails them. Christianity has become an institution competing with other secular institutions for power. And power for Erika Mitterer means what it meant for Jacob Burckhardt: absolute evil.

In reading Berchtold Gierer's narrative (*Geschlechter am See*) about medieval life around Lake Constance, in the countryside and in the small towns on both sides of the lake and of the Rhine, we are beset with a similar sense of a life heavy with frustration, brutality, and unpredictable evil interference. Again the Church is made the scapegoat for most of the insecurity and arbitrariness from which common people suffer; a ray of hope glows faintly from the cities with their freedom-loving artisans and merchants.

Erika Mitterer speaks of power as the Prince of the World; Gierer calls those in possession of power the Gods of the World. There is little difference in their terminology, and none in the meaning underlying it. The Powers that be, in Gierer's characterization, wind like threatening shadows along the streets, frightening people in their dreams. They are the nightmares, the weeping sound of the bell ringing for an execution, the moaning of those held in the clutches of the torturer, the groans of dying men. These Powers abuse the anxiety of enslaved people, they whisper into each person's ear the calumnies he is to hurl against his neighbour.

This insecurity of the medieval period is described for North Germany, in the same grey hues, by Hans Leip (*Das Muschelhorn*). His picture is of Hamburg, a city which, unlike the South German towns in Gierer's and Erika Mitterer's novels, at least has the sea as a road of escape, as a gateway to a freer world. But the advantage is offset by the fact that the same sea sends out its own oppressors in the form of predatory brigands. "Times were dull, life monotonous, oppressed by the fear of magistrates and sin, threatened everywhere by robbers, plagues, superstition, and devilry. A few were happy, and those who were rich enough to be happy made one another miserable with their conceit, greed, gluttony, quarrels, calumnies, lawsuits, and executions. Yet those who pretended to have chosen a life of inner contentment, the clerics above all, were, with few exceptions, not different, and those who were honest with themselves and with the world were tortured by doubts."

There is, of course, the possibility that the Reformation, the incipient stages of which Leip records, will bring the longed-for riddance from fear, and that the Wittenberg volcano, Martin Luther, will have enough sense to grasp the pure, fiery meaning of the Gospels, "to discard the ingredients added to them by those who use war and peace as equally convenient excuses for holding mankind in fetters." The silver lining of hope is there; in the meantime people have to live as best they can.

Of a multitude of characters who are being tossed about by the despotic will of secular and spiritual rulers, two stand out for their endeavour to fight free of their oppressors. Imel Abdena, the one-time chieftain of independence-loving Frisians, recognizes no authority except his own. A freebooter challenging the growing power and influence of the Hanse merchants, he overreaches himself in the fashion of the ancient *hubris* and has to spend the rest of his life in a dungeon. Only a brief success is given by the author to the inveterate egotist who tries to forestall the authorities by taking the law into his own hands. Leip's sympathy is clearly with the more peaceful counterpart to Imel, a sculptor who endeavours to lead an existence devoted to the creation and enjoyment of art. Contemplation is to be preferred to excessive and ruthless activity; solace comes only to him who can withdraw from the arbitrariness and insecurity of the world. The humanist scholars in Erika Mitterer's book have much the same philosophy. There is, in her novel and in Leip's, a gap that ought to have been filled by the social and political reformer. Prudence may have cautioned both authors to leave the gap.

If we lift the episode of Imel Abdena's rebellion out of its context, we have one more of the many dictator stories which the period under review has produced. Of these *Auf den Marmor-klippen,* by Ernst Jünger, has received a good deal of critical attention and praise inside Germany and even more in other countries. On the strength of this slender volume the author was, during the war, taken note of as a *frondeur* to be watched and to be remembered in due time: he is now considered by many the man of destiny in the literature of the reconstruction period.

A credulous Swiss journalist not long ago told the world that Jünger had assured him he was not, when working on the *Marmorklippen,* thinking of Hitler Germany. But it is as impossible for a reader of the book not to relate its condensed horrors to places and instances of modern brutality, as it must have been for the author to devise such blood-stained symbols without reference to actuality. A period such as Germany has gone through could not fail to produce horror-filled imaginations; the only question was whether these imaginations would, among the many outlets open to them, find that of the imagery of literary presentation. We now know that they have done so in several cases, of which *Auf den Marmorklippen* is but the one that has attracted the greatest attention.

The mood created by dictator stories is determined by the ravages of the monster described, and by the manner in which the outside world is shown to react to them.

Margot Boger (*Die goldene Maske*) tells of a legendary clan in the environs of Rome, and of their chief, whose excesses in brutality she could hardly have recounted without recourse to contemporary history. But since the hatred of this beast spends itself on his own immediate *entourage* and in a feud against his city relatives (all birds of a feather) the danger of this dictator character seems somehow contained. Moreover, the author leaves no doubt that the obsolete vitality of her bloodhound hero carries its own doom with it. "His playing with forces which for centuries

have forfeited their right to exist was bound to turn out a boome-
rang; an end would have to come." For Germans under National
Socialism to read this and other denunciations of dictatorial
arbitrariness, and to see the forecast of an ignominious end
promptly fulfilled, must have been a strange experience, hope-
fully accepted by some, indignantly rejected by others.

Yüan Schi-Kai, by Ernst Wurm, leaves a much more ambiguous impression in the mind of the reader. For the author has no
sooner brought this Chinese dictator down on his knees, than he
proclaims the advent of a whole group of usurpers on the Chinese
coast, namely the Japanese invaders, driven, so we are told, by a
sense of a task too lofty to be comprehended by Anglo-Saxon
shopkeepers, and equally incomprehensible to the dreamy
Chinese. "Our creative impulse lies in the marching step of our
nation, it is motion for the sake of motion." Is this an attempt to
silence with a final flourish official German criticism, just in case
the Yüan Schi-Kai part of the book should be suspected to be
a frank attack on dictatorship? Or does the author wish to
insinuate that there is no end to these locust conquerors, and that
peace-loving people are forever at their mercy? As it is, the book
rejects one form of totalitarianism to welcome another, and the
author will find it hard to make us believe that in his innermost
thoughts he wanted to reject both.

There can be no doubt that the circumstances of literary
activity under National Socialism were such that on occasion the
employment of strange devices and subterfuges became necessary.
It will take time, and more accurate information, to define in
every case the nexus between literary intention and artistic expression. *Auf den Marmorklippen* will tempt many a literary
scholar to try to unravel its knot of symbols; so will Herta Snell's
novel *Abenteuer in Kyparissia.*

The latter is a strangely moving tale about the transgressions
of a legendary duke Makrynos; he has murdered the husband of
beautiful Myrtane, and kidnapped the widow's two sons in order
to extract a promise of marriage from her. Fortunatus, a chance
arrival on his island, is able to liberate the children and force

the tyrant to leave the country, thus restoring justice and confidence among the perturbed inhabitants. Written in a genuinely personal style which is yet never startlingly original, the novel slowly but steadily spreads a mood of anxiety which, however, then recedes before the forces of intelligence, tolerance, patience, and Christian sympathy. The evil is counteracted and defeated, not with brutal weapons, but with rational action growing out of the will to justice and kindness.

While the dictator-duke is not the black scoundrel which rumour and the unqualified description of his conduct make him out to be, what he has done remains condemnable and calls for his removal. For psychological understanding should not be tantamount to forgiveness and indulgence.

Once the myth of Makrynos the invincible demon has been exploded, everybody sees that he was not the man to live in a sphere beyond good and evil. There is, in fact, no such man, for "everyone is responsible for his deeds and will have to account for them." The lesson that crime does not pay was the first point to be driven home; Herta Snell makes it her second concern to show a true leader. It is not only for his exploit, the exposure of the duke, that Fortunatus is mentioned as his successor, for even this exploit was not entirely made of heroic stuff but had its all-too-human ingredients. He is really predestined to a position of the greatest responsibility, such as that of a ruler (if not in Kyparissia then somewhere else, provided that extraordinary circumstances should call for the appointment of a leader), by his spiritual qualities and social virtues: intelligence, consideration for others, compassion. Makrynos is a deplorable incident in the history of the island which should not make the inhabitants pessimistic about the possibility of truly public-spirited men. This is the message of hope that supersedes the gloom of the opening chapters.

Something similar happens in Jünger's dictator novel, where the flood of violence is also made to abate, in the end, to be remembered as an unfortunate interlude, while new confidence in life rises. Yet this confidence is not the confidence that reappears in the closing pages of Herta Snell's book. Jünger raises no definite hope for an orderly world in which society as a whole can live peacefully. His world is populated partly by wild hordes, partly by small, select groups of people, such as those to which the botanist-scholar narrator or the patriarchal farmers belong. It is these small groups rather than a large and compact society which the destructive forces of the Lemures and Mauretanians menace. And these groups have become resigned to the occasional outbreak of unchecked brutality; they look upon a quiet day as a gift to be enjoyed and to be consumed quickly, for tomorrow disaster may catch up with them again. "And even sweeter is the memory of our moon and sun years when sudden terror has been putting an end to them. Then only do we realize how fortunate we human beings are to be allowed to live within our small communities, under a peaceful roof, with good conversation, and with friendly greetings in the morning and at night. Alas, too late do we realize that in granting us such gifts fate is giving abundantly." It is this precarious life, with nothing better to look forward to, which is resumed after the storm has passed. Once again there is a roof overhead, the sun shines, and men and women gather in freedom, now more than before conscious that this is all they can hope for. This being the case, it is not surprising that some individuals, those who have drawn deeply from the changeability of existence, are not only prepared to witness the loss of all the fruits of their labour, as the botanist-scholars are, but can even watch the oncoming catastrophe with a sense of philosophical or aesthetic disengagement as a phenomenon that is natural to social life and bound to recur from time to time. From here it is only a short step to an acceptance of even the worst calamities as part of a cosmic *coincidentia oppositorum*. Herta Snell, who shows excellent psychological penetration into the nature of evil, yet does not accept it; her world is striving and perhaps moving towards a higher life of permanent peace and social order.

The impression that Jünger is willing to compromise, if not with the Lemures and Mauretanians, then at least with less violent forms of power, is strengthened by an essay[1] in which he concedes that *désinvolture* takes the sting out of power. "Man

[1]"Zur Désinvolture"; in *Das abenteuerliche Herz,* 1938/42.

is after all more than a beast, he is the master of all beasts." We are, Jünger asserts, too much inclined to associate power with will. There is another kind of power that we possess and exercise by virtue of good fortune befalling us, or by virtue of some magic touch that gives us power over others. Power of this description has its irresistible charm, as it had with Louis XIV. *Auf den Marmorklippen* contains one character with such power, old Bolivar, an absolute ruler within the precincts of his family and his vast holdings, and for all except Jünger indistinguishable from a budding tyrant.

For Erika Mitterer, Gierer, and Leip the feeling of *Angst* is less an existential and more an historical phenomenon, the result of unfortunate but temporary conditions. Jünger, on the other hand, would hold us to a mood of perpetual fear; while rejoicing that one storm has blown over, we must be prepared for another now brewing.

It is one of the great attractions of Werner Bergengruen's novel *Am Himmel wie auf Erden* that it combines belief in the existential nature of *Angst* with a firm conviction that man can be taught to control this most depressing phenomenon. Bergengruen's book bears some resemblance to those of Leip, Gierer, and Erika Mitterer. The period he treats is close to that of the *Muschelhorn,* of *Geschlechter am See* and *Der Fürst der Welt,* the early sixteenth century, with the illustrations taken this time from Berlin and the surrounding districts. Moreover, some of the anxieties gripping the population are the result of purely historical, temporary conditions, the arbitrary government of the Elector, for instance, and, even more important, a panicky belief (growing out of the prophecy of one Professor Stöffler in Tübingen) that in 1524 a new flood will rise and wipe out all vestiges of human life in the lowlands.

But these few similarities must not be allowed to overshadow a basic difference. Bergengruen knows of another source of *Angst,* of a fear so powerful and elemental that one of the characters comes to the conclusion that the flood would be a merciful event, after all, in view of this fundamental misery which is inherent in life. Such existential fear normally reaches our consciousness after the protective layer of childhood beliefs has withered away. "That our parents are leaving us is the surest indication of the fact that within the sphere of earthly existence there will be no one and nothing to relieve us of fear," Bergengruen says, and it will require a special effort before this statement can be qualified. Elemental *Angst,* in this novel, appears in the form of a fear of leprosy, an ever-present apprehension that you or I might be the next one to develop the symptoms, and to be cast out into the pitiful, sub-human mob of lepers. Needless to say, the particular affliction is meant to symbolize illness and misery in general, the onslaught of some great misfortune (and there is always one waiting in ambush) that will deprive us of our human features and deny us the right to live in normal society.

However, in the end Bergengruen is able to show that if the source of such fear is immanent in existence, there is also inherent provision for a remedy that will conquer it. This remedy lies in courage, love, and spiritual discipline. Those who have risen above fear must then teach others to live without it, to enjoy the compensations available to us—the blessings of art, science, and social life—to become masters of their passions and servants of justice, truth, and love.

The dialectics of evolution work no less for moods and emotions than for ideas. Under any except the most strained conditions it could be taken for granted that the spread of gloom, in one part of the literary world, would in another produce its humorous or satirical antithesis. Literary expression was however not free enough to follow its natural bent, at least not its satirical bent. To write successful satire it is first of all necessary to attack an object that deserves ridicule. It is obvious that Fritz Spiesser was ambitious to produce the great satirical novel of our time; unfortunately he wasted a fair measure of intellectual and literary ability by placing himself on the wrong side of the fence. His *Westliche Robinsonade,* instead of satirizing the Third Reich, rushes to its literary succour and tries to poke fun at democracy.

This is not to deny that, in ridiculing the efforts of a group of sailors marooned on a tiny island to rebuild their fortunes on the basis of fraternity and equality, Spiesser brings to light a few human and institutional weaknesses. Yet notwithstanding their occasional mistakes, these amateur law-makers are fundamentally right, whereas the author is basically wrong. His distortions only tend to emphasize how much in the wrong he is. The laughter he wants to produce congeals on our lips into something akin to disgust and horror at such impudently displayed political obscurantism. The reader feels constantly impelled to protect the victims of his satirical stabs. As a document recording all the clumsy half-truths and irrational aberrations that were used by the enemies of sound reasoning to malign freedom of thought and of discussion, Spiesser's novel ought to serve future historians well.

If vital satire was out of the question in Germany under Hitler (a few drops of vitriol in Editha Klipstein's *Der Zuschauer,* and in Ottfried Graf Finckenstein's *Dämmerung* may indicate how far an author could go without forfeiting his right to publish or to live), all types of tepid humour fared, of course, much better. The humorous current in German writing, never as thin as foreign observers are apt to declare it to be, was far from disappearing in the past few years. In dialect literature it was probably as strong as ever. Its appearance in High German seems to have been determined by one condition only, that of the talent available.[1] The recent crop of self-styled humorous novels is impressive in quantity, yet their aggregate hilarity is far surpassed in a novel not declared to be humorous, *Die sanfte Gewalt* by Bruno Brehm.

Brehm has the gift, so rarely possessed by the habitual fun-makers, for enticing us to laugh without manifestly compelling us to do so. He seems merely to release the humour that is inherent in some situation, or in some characters. It is not too much to say

[1]Heinrich Spoerl apparently enjoyed a great reputation as a humorist, though he was never able to repeat the well-deserved success of his excellent farce *Die Feuerzangenbowle* (1923).

that in *Die sanfte Gewalt* the serenity of a traditionally serene people, the Austrians, has once again crystallized into artistic expression, into literary expression this time whereas the last great manifestation happened to come through the medium of music, the music of Mozart. If it were a slightly cruder form of humour an idea of it could be conveyed by briefly indicating the contents of the novel. The scene is Austria before the turn of the last century, and the story concerns two officer friends who have fallen in love and have to extricate each other from adverse conditions threatening their happiness. As it is, the factual elements, among which the visit of an exotic potentate to the Hapsburg dignitaries is to be included, rather than being squeezed for comic situations, are part and parcel of a substance that radiates, with varying degrees of intensity, an incessant glow of serenity. This mood is so strong that it forms the *raison d'être* of the novel and provides it with both plot and problem. A serene, tranquil mind, so we learn, helps to solve our human problems, leaving only one major concern, how to protect this serenity from the corroding influence of vulgar reality. Brehm offers no solution, unless it be contained in his tacit invitation to escape into a world of art such as his own books create. Even such a limited lesson has its value and should not be wholly lost sight of in the turmoil of life.

10 *Entertainment*

THE main purpose of this commentary has been to throw some light on the problems discussed in German novels of recent years and on the fundamental moods they display. If a considerable number of the books studied go unmentioned, because they are not good enough, or not bad enough, to call for comment, this does not imply that they all fail to raise a problem of some kind or other, but that the problems presented are of a rather indifferent kind, or treated in an indifferent way. They were found to be too light, though "lightness" in the German novel has a connotation all its own.

A classification of the novels that can be dismissed as not relevant enough, according to content, which is the only sensible classification in view of the lack of formal distinction, makes it apparent that most of these lighter novels are the backwash from the discussions of subjects indicated in the headings of the preceding chapters. Peasant novels outnumber all others, though historical fiction comes a close second. The exploits of German and other Nordic warriors, in the olden days, receive much attention. The Nibelungs and Vikings, the Vandals, Franks, Helvetians, and Merovingians have all found their enthusiastic bards. Next in historical chronology come a number of works extolling the virtues of such pure-bred German leaders as Widukind, or the Old Saxon king Heinrich, or Otto I, as well as minor figures from the long fight between German secular rulers and Roman ecclesiastics. A few authors here leave the beaten track of military and political history to accompany the early pioneers trekking from North Germany and Flanders into the Silesian hills. Stories featuring life among the Teutonic Knights, or in the Hanse cities of the sixteenth century seem to be as popular as ever. In chapter

IX reference was made to the dark moods suggested by early and late medieval times; typically enough, these moods are also found in less pretentious literature. Coming to the Reformation and the Counter-Reformation, we notice a few novels dealing with the Anabaptists, the rebellious peasants of South Germany, and the expulsion of the Salzburg Protestants, and with such figures as the alchemist Thurneysser, the soldier of fortune Frundsberg, and the Salzburg archbishop Wolf Dietrich (the latter also qualifies as a prototype of the ruthless dictator who ends his life in prison). The Seven Years' War, and especially the Napoleonic Wars and the Congress of Vienna, provide an inexhaustible treasure of incidents for the rank and file of novelists who with one exception (a novel about Scharnhorst by Mirko Jelusich, *Der Soldat*) choose their period for its stage-property value rather than for any genuinely historical problems which it might raise. The same is, of course, true of the First World War which must have been considered interesting material while the Second World War was raging. Needless to say, even events around 1940 have, in a few instances, been worked up into semi-historical fiction. What sampling was possible among the latter may not have discovered the general trend, yet it is only fair to say that the mental worries of those left behind are given at least as much consideration as the triumphant elation of successful aggression. A small proportion of historical novels choose their subjects from such foreign fields and figures as Alexander the Great, the Byzantine empress Theophano, Mohammed the Second, the conqueror of the Byzantine empire, old Peru, Venice, Charles the Bold of Burgundy, Cesare Borgia, James II of England, and the beginnings of the East Indian Trading Company. In two novels President Kruger is made to serve the ends of anti-British propaganda.

Interest in art and the artist likewise extends from higher to lower literary levels. The works discussed in chapter v have a long line of successors in which the subject-matter remains the same, much as the literary quality may have deteriorated. Historical artist characters (Walther von der Vogelweide, Villon, Bacon-Shakespeare, Fischer von Erlach, Rubens, Swift, Seume, Bellman,

Caroline von Schlegel, Mozart, Wagner, Grieg, Annette von Droste-Hülshoff) and fictitious musicians, painters, and poets are evenly represented.

Medicine, foreign nations, and education must also be added to the list of topics that figure prominently in novels which on any other standard than that of content would rate as wholly insignificant. It is of course a typical ambition of German writers to be considered strong on the side of content, and, indeed, while the intellectual power to discuss a problem pungently is quite often lacking in these lesser writers, we must in many cases at least admit the presence of good and serious intentions. It is when the absence of both intelligence and effort is covered up with false pretences, that the German idiosyncrasy about profound content turns into a preposterous sham.

Progressive critics aware of the sociological implications of literature have long felt that the German tradition of saturating fiction with philosophy (pseudo-philosophy it was in many instances) arose from a delusion with regard to the true wishes of the public, and that the supply exceeded the demand by far. It can in any case be taken for granted that German readers, like the readers of other literatures, are from time to time desirous of material that is not primarily thought-provoking, but absorbingly entertaining. How is this demand being met?

Before and during the reign of Hitler, Germans had their writers whose sole aim it was to produce, sell, and make money on books that entertained, and, if they posed problems, did so for no other purpose than that of creating additional interest. The ways in which they did this even from 1939 to 1944 are not much different from those pursued in other countries, except that detective stories were never very popular in Germany. Subject-matter was limited to the well-known themes of assured entertainment value: the man who stands between two women; the old bachelor who all of a sudden decides to find himself a spouse; father and son (or two close friends) who are rivals in love; the Enoch Arden constellation, the solution of which is in one case happily varied when the second husband and his wife stay on good terms with the first husband; the gypsy girl and her upper-class lover whose faith is rewarded when it is established that she is really of a higher class too; the meandering husband who ruefully returns to his wife; death dissolving an unhappy union and leaving the surviving partner to find true, though belated bliss. Again, a fairly large number of these second-rate novels are generation novels following the vicissitudes of a family through fifty or a hundred years. Football players and movie actors figure as heroes in a few instances; now and then we are introduced into the milieu of circus and vaudeville artists. There was enough paper, in 1942, to fill more than 500 pages with the strip-tease technique of a Viennese girl who falls foul of the morality squad. The first erotic experiences of students, with happy or tragic results, are a perennial drawing-card of the literature of entertainment; they reappear here, flavoured by a moralizing attitude that would have met with the approval of the Victorians. These time-honoured themes remain favoured subjects, and the current political situation is only rarely dealt with; when it is, National Socialism usually acts the part of a fairy godmother who, if embraced, will remove some obstacle between two lovers. If there is no cause for elation about the craftsmanship of these books, one experiences, on the other hand, a hilarious gratification over the fact that countless readers, behind the backs of their political leaders, their uplifters and reformers, obviously went on reading trash of the type that their parents and their grandparents had turned to for relaxation. Thus official orders were ignored at both the top and the bottom layers of recent German fiction.

A handful of writers, too conscious of their responsibility ever to produce chaff, yet not bold enough to face the opposition squarely, found a very ingenious way of preserving their artistic and personal integrity under the disguise of a light, entertaining type of fiction, by writing about their childhood and youth.[1] And,

[1] Wilhelm Pleyer, *Tal der Kindheit*; E. von Alten, *Kindersommer*; Hans Leip, *Jan Himp und die kleine Brise*; Josef Magnus Wehner, *Erste Liebe*; Josef Wenter, *Leise, leise! liebe Quelle*.

as if the demand had exceeded the current supply, older works transposing the reader into the enchanted land of youth were reprinted during the war, as for instance Emil Barth's *Das verlorene Haus* (1936) and Wilhelm Schmidtbonn's *An einem Strom geboren* (1935). These two books, in addition to the sheer delight they gave, must have helped thousands of people to escape despair over prevailing conditions and to build a sanctuary where, disguised as childhood reminiscences, much of a valuable tradition, literary and human, could be stored and resorted to for spiritual comfort and hope.

11 The Western Tradition

IT IS, for the time being, impossible to say what proportion of the total output of German novels from 1939 to 1944 this selection (some 400 books) represents. Even in the worst case—if the novels not seen should all belong to the blood and soil type or be works conceived by such debased minds as Eggers' or such simpletons as Bürkle—it would still be true that a respectable literary tradition was never quite extinct. A number of the novels discussed bear no marks of the régime under which they were written, or at any rate published and, we hope, read. If there are on occasion disquieting symptoms, a preference for vague idealization or mystification, or manifestations of social apathy, it must be remembered that these are characteristic shortcomings in German literature which date back centuries. Their correction, a more comprehensive objectivity and a greater sympathy with men, may well come out of the tradition itself, as has happened from time to time in the past, through the works of Reuter, Gotthelf, Keller, Hauptmann, and others. For the moment, we must be content to see that the tradition as it persisted through the nineteenth century has survived and may well be strengthened again. Its imperfection is of a kind that responds to treatment and therefore need not worry us too much, as long as we know that the danger of total destruction has been averted.

A number of authors worth noting for their integrity appear to be novices whose names were not known before the war to students of German literature. If their personal record is as good as their literary reputation, they should be heard of again. It is equally gratifying to see that the oldest generation of writers still active, men born in the sixties and seventies of the last century such as Weigand, Stehr, Strauss, Carossa, Winnig, Claudius (and the slightly younger von der Trenck), have made few concessions to their political masters. Or, to put it more cautiously and to allow for possible surprises once we get more information about their personal or literary conduct, each of the authors mentioned published during the war at least one book that flowers from past traditions.

Carossa, Stehr, and Winnig published works that continued or, in Stehr's case, completed a series of novels begun long before. In none of these instances do we get the impression that an original plan was interfered with or patently modified under pressure of political exigencies. *Damian* by Hermann Stehr, the last volume of the Maechler trilogy, brings the history of the family up to the years of the Weimar Republic.[1] Stehr carries forward into this volume all the mystifying gadgets of spookish powers that had such a disproportionately strong influence over the thoughts and actions of Damian's father and grandfather. What saves this hocus-pocus from becoming its own parody is the fact that the First World War, and even more the demands of the period immediately following it, force Stehr to wrestle with issues more pressing than those of the spiritualistic heirlooms of the Maechler family. For once a Maechler scion seems to be able to throw off an obsession with introspection; he becomes indeed a political leader and the head of a people's council which takes over the municipal authority after the collapse, in order to guarantee a measure of normal communal life and to provide food and other necessities. Remembering what a decisive stage the Weimar Republic was for the heroes of German educational novels, we at once wonder how Damian will face the crisis. His first steps are taken in the right direction of active participation and genuine devotion to social tasks. But we are soon disappointed. Damian, after he has suffered a few setbacks such as would only fire a strong man to even greater efforts, withdraws from public life to fall back not so much on the pathological morbidity of the family tradition as on religious mysticism and indi-

[1]For a searching analysis of this posthumously published novel see Karl S. Weimar, *"Damian," Monatshefte,* XXXVIII (1946).

vidualism. Though Damian is a serious student of classical culture and is well on his way to a university appointment, this does not in any way prevent him from abandoning his interest in society for ruminations about the necessity of perfecting oneself. "To act and to live our lives in accordance with this sacred egoism, with this human-divine individualism, the only form of individualism to which man is entitled, because its obligations are world-wide, brings into play the true, genuine, and living spirit of collectivism, an attitude which of course is automatically identified with democracy, with that ideal of an eternal humanity which is the meaning and the measure of all things."

Here as in many other passages of similar spiritual loftiness our quarrel is not with the words and with their well-meant intentions, but with the lack of application to a concrete situation. Instead of leading Damian back into the fold of social, collective life, Stehr makes matters worse by conjuring up an even more verbose mystic than Damian, a character who roams through others of Stehr's novels and who now turns this one into an orgy of idealism and mysticism. It is highly revealing that the crisis of the post-war period is left for this fictitious Faber to solve, just as in *Der Heiligenhof* he was invoked to settle a strike among the Ruhr miners. Yet neither here nor there does Faber amount to more than a legendary shadow; his rhapsodic lyricism, in spite of all the edification Stehr's characters pretend to receive from it, leaves us bewildered and with a sense of being cheated out of a clear-cut decision.

The unsatisfactory end of *Damian* is not the result of National Socialism, which has hardly affected the author, as far as his last novel is concerned. But it is very likely that had it not been for the appearance of National Socialism we should be less keenly aware of the traditional idiosyncrasy of so many German intellectuals to save an individual and to let society fend for itself.

Another work completed or at least carried on during the war is Carossa's poetical autobiography. *Das Jahr der schönen Täuschungen* begins where *Verwandlungen einer Jugend* (1928) left off. The scene shifts to Munich where young Carossa now starts his medical studies. Much as we hear of his thrilling intellectual encounters with medicine and with chemistry at the university, and of his explorations of the social life of the city, the country-side is never far away, for it is needed to satisfy Carossa's persistent and characteristic longing for harmonious living. Even in these student years his contemplative tranquillity always helps him to confine experience to the function of feeding his creative impulse. With an inborn belief in the healing faculty of nature, Carossa is ever ready to make light of any difficulties, and to recover from whatever shocks his youthful soul may suffer. The story is as thoroughly impregnated as its predecessors with the Goethe-Stifter tradition. Hence it remained impervious to National Socialistic pressure. There is not a jarring note in its variations upon a modern theodicy. One moment of apprehension, on the second last page of the book, is quickly relieved: during the holidays young Carossa by chance wanders through a district in which the annual manoeuvres are being held; on reaching his home he tells his father of a compelling desire to become an officer. The doctor father gently talks him out of it, reminding his son of an army to which he, as a medical student, already belongs, the medical profession, which even in peace-time is continuously confronted with the most powerful enemies.

The work calls for a continuation, and, if produced, this will most likely take Carossa's classicism into the reconstruction period. While it cannot be expected that the author, at his advanced age, will revitalize this tradition for the needs of our time, he will at any rate stand out as a model of commendable literary integrity.

In recapitulating the days of his wanderings as a travelling journeyman (*Das Buch Wanderschaft*), August Winnig fills, as a postscript informs us, some gaps that his earlier books had left. We are naturally prepared to see him put into these gaps pre-dated National Socialistic ideas. Winnig's rank as a writer is not important enough to merit much attention for his book; still less are we attracted to it by his personal reputation, for his political record is rather unsavoury. Yet if we knew nothing about the past of this renegade socialist, unstinted praise for this autobiographical account would be in order. For the reminiscences are varied and unaffected by later changes in Winnig's political attitude. One cannot help feeling that the author roams through these interesting years of hardships and bitter economic struggles, in which he does not lose a Bohemian light-heartedness and an irrepressible, wholesome merriment, as if through a paradise lost. Those were the years in which he felt elated by a deep sympathy for the workers and by unswerving loyalty to the cause of humanity, with no shadows of a subsequent betrayal hanging over him. True enough, the book ends with a report of Winnig's discussion of the workers' movement with a dissident socialist who warns him that the present state of society cannot for long allow the demand for untrammelled freedom, and that a check will have to be applied if society as a whole is to benefit from progressive attitudes. However, Winnig does not claim that National Socialism was the correction his friend envisaged. This may or may not be a tacit admission on the part of the author that the nationalist remedy proved wrong; the fact remains that his obvious and undiluted joy in living comes to an end when he begins to dissociate himself from the socialist movement, and that is exactly as far as his reminiscences take us.

Wilhelm Weigand and Emil Strauss have long shared the honour of being among the most accomplished masters of the craft of story-telling. Conscious of the artistic possibilities that lie in a harmonious interplay of formal and technical dexterity with imagination, they prefer freedom of invention to the constraint imposed by too much autobiographical reference. They draw less on the actual events of their own lives and more on the insight and wisdom derived therefrom. Their latest books are no exception and follow again this method which is objective, and yet alive with personality.

Strauss can never conceal his Alamannic temperament, which injects itself into his plots and characters. In *Lebenstanz* this happens to such an extent that it not only dates but also mars an otherwise classically trimmed theme, the story of a jilted lover who comes back after many years to woo again his former sweetheart, now a divorced woman in her forties, whose happiness as well as his own the hero restores. The dating is quite in order: the First World War and the difficulties after 1918 are fittingly introduced as events that might well have turned thoughtful people into mature characters, who can forget past mistakes and join hands again, to work for a better future. Dr. Durban, a timid high-school teacher who was easily out-distanced by a superficially brilliant competitor, develops a personality that faces life, first abroad and then during the war as a soldier, with unflinching courage. That he afterwards should mentally prepare himself, and the reader, for the coming of a strong man who will oust the Marxists, put the Jews out of business, and give free rein to German dynamism, spoils the story for posterity. Strauss is, of course, too much an artist to let a vigorously conceived development of character bog down in party politics and day-to-day political quarrels; he mentions none of the leaders in the background by name, and he makes no effort to describe in any but the vaguest terms the infiltration of National Socialistic propaganda into the country-side of southern Germany. Yet in another way Strauss incriminates himself even more, by a painfully blunt renunciation of intellectual acumen in favour of a mystic irrationalism. For all his education and experience in foreign countries, Dr. Durban remains wedded to the belief that the Germans are different from all other peoples, and that this difference is their proudest distinction: they are unique in that they are satisfied to go on living joyfully and striving zealously, even if no rational goal will ever come into sight. "No sooner have our longings to give form to things, our life-planning activism, our purposeful aim launched into the flowing and ebbing sea of existence, than they turn into an unexpected fairy-tale and all our forces are pressed into the service of strange and unknown goals; as long as the will with which we set out remains with us, we have achieved enough." This is as unequivocal an acceptance and recommendation of the pattern of aimless striving as German irrationalists have ever advocated.

Der Ruf am Morgen, by Wilhelm Weigand, though designated a novel, is a collection of stories arranged in cyclical form with a framework story as the platter on which the literary delicacies are served. Though the reader will soon enough discover the similarity of this work to Keller's *Sinngedicht,* and continue to the very end noticing features common to the two books, he will not deny Weigand a mastery all his own and a very marked originality. If, as the author says, it took him from 1916 to 1940 to complete this work, his application was well rewarded, for the result is little short of a great piece of literature. Such it may indeed still become. Its chief fault is that it was not written in the nineteenth century, for with such a date it would not have been expected to deal with strictly current problems. With equal justification it can be held that some time in the future *Der Ruf am Morgen* will move into a much higher literary position; a time may well come again when we shall feel more inclined than we do now to be absorbed by the more general, timeless problems of human character and by fundamental human situations, especially the test to which love puts men and women. It is of the latter that Weigand tells, by creating characters and conditions that are recurrent in Western civilization: a timid philosopher not bold enough to love and to capture the prize of love, when the opportunity presents itself; an actor who in his vain ambition cannot resist the temptation to use his future father-in-law as a comic model, and who thus loses the affection of his sweetheart while gaining some ephemeral success on the stage; the inexperienced young woman seduced by an irresponsible sensualist, but saved by a mature man who loves her and defies conventional prejudices; a spoilt girl who is in love with a struggling musician, but prefers an easy life at the side of a wealthy nonentity to a common fight for higher ideals; the woman who when forced to choose between two rivals, one a bold good-for-nothing, the other a successful if pedantic *bourgeois,* takes the latter as a husband but retains the former as her lover. These and other groups keep up, for one night, the discussion about the problems of life, and especially about the nature of human conscience. The answer to the main problem, the nature of real love, is given in the framework story, in which a young man and his girl, after a temporary alienation caused by the man's difficulty in adjusting himself to normal life when the horrors of the battle-field fill his memory, are reunited. The great experience that brings about their reconciliation is their realization that life is a serious business which must not be trifled with; true joy of living and the crowning bliss of love come only to those who are deeply conscious of and grateful for the miracle of existence.

Life with its many imperishable riches, and the right way to find these, form the theme of yet another novel written by a seasoned German writer. Siegfried von der Trenck, in *Reichardt aus der Fülle,* shares with Weigand an exuberant zeal for the acquisition of culture and a great reverence for all intellectual creativeness. Weigand surveys human destiny with calm serenity, but von der Trenck makes forays impetuously into cultural terri-tories. Also, unlike Weigand again, who speaks for a common European culture, von der Trenck, though not narrowly national, draws more exclusively from German sources, notably from Kant, Goethe, Schiller, and Nietzsche. The hero of the story, a student in economics, is interested only in the best that tradition can offer; from Kant he takes not so much the categorical im-perative as the stoic optimism displayed in the treatise *Von der Macht des Gemüts,* from Goethe an objectivity that bids us accept the world and work on it, to refine it. But at the same time the young student is convinced that the Germans are vicariously called upon to help the white man retain cultural leadership. France missed her chance to become the champion of Western civilization when during the Revolution she produced leaders who were strong in blind hatred and so weak in sympathy and love. England, through Darwin, presented the hypothesis of man's evolution from the animals. Though this may be acceptable historically, the English made a fatal mistake when they not only proclaimed the unalterable fact of man's preying nature but en-couraged him to develop it. They should have arrived at the opposite conclusion: that man must strive to overcome the initial handicap of his animal origin. Though in other respects critical of Nietzsche, von der Trenck thinks he has, as the prophet of the superman, assigned to Germany the most important task for centuries to come. Once Nietzsche had expounded his conception of man, "there was no longer only one creator who had, at one time, created the world, and human beings were no longer creations only; they had, at least some of them, and each with his own task, been planted in the world to be creators themselves."

The author does not seriously attempt to elaborate any creative participation of his hero. With the kind of inconclusive practical result that provides an ending for the book we are only too familiar. The theoretical decision, however, is clear enough: it is made in favour of the creative superman, of a dynamism that goes out into life to change it and to experiment with it, and against Schopenhauer's quietism. To leave no doubt about the inadvisability, for Germans, of becoming devout Christians, von der Trenck expressly declares the teachings of Christ to be the fruit of Eastern softness, of an extreme self-surrender which could only be taught among people who were in no danger of taking it seriously. "If white people on occasion tried to live in strict accordance with the Gospels, they paid for it with their extinction."

This is the most outspoken abrogation of Christianity, as far as the oldest generation of present-day German writers is concerned. At least in theory, all connexion with the Christian tradition is severed, though the hero in von der Trenck's novel really does nothing a tolerant Christian could not condone. Other representatives of this older generation are mostly non-committal with regard to Christianity. Strauss remarks in passing that neither Christ nor Buddha reached the goal they had set for themselves. On another occasion he points to the difference in character between Christ and the disciples; the former was hearty, serious, warm-hearted, and serene, accepting and enjoying reality, whereas the latter became fanatics, ascetics, idealists of a kind that uses men as mere means to some esoteric purpose. For Stehr, Christ is one of the great teachers of mankind, along with

Plato, Buddha, Lao-tze, Eckhart. Christianity, if it is not dead as an institution, has at any rate lost all idealism. "Serious-minded people all over the world know that Jesus of Nazareth, whom they call the first Christian, had no thought of establishing a church. They know that the insight of this mythical man dwelt in the fire of an idealism which purified the demands of individualism to such an extent that they became the commandments of God. . . . Because it contradicted the imperialistic instincts of the Church, the word of the man from Nazareth was suppressed, though it gives voice to the deepest aspiration of men—the Kingdom of Heaven is within you—a conviction which forms the life-blood of Buddha's teachings as it does of those of Lao-tze, and to which Emerson and Kant have paid homage." Christ's message is for Stehr a stepping-stone to a new individualism which, as was pointed out earlier, is too much enshrouded in mysticism to qualify even as Christian humanism. Winnig, writing the autobiography of a young worker whose interest is fully absorbed by the problems of his job and of his class, does not, of course, deal with religious matters. Yet for all that, Winnig and even von der Trenck, and of course Carossa whose books are tinged with Catholic lore, all belong to the Western tradition whose tenets they partly accept and partly modify.

How does the new generation compare with the older on this question of philosophical-religious beliefs? It is easy to see that von der Trenck's faith in a new conception of man, the superman, links him closely with some of the younger advocates of German "energism." However, there is reason to assume that these advocates form a minority, if not a quantitative then at least a qualitative minority. In chapter ix it has been shown that quite a few writers, good writers at that, are on a serious quest for Christian or more broadly humanistic ethics that can be applied to the conduct of life. These writers are closer to Western traditions than their elders. One might almost speak of a very distinct hiatus segregating an older, sceptical generation from a new school that is deeply concerned with the revitalization of Christianity, or at any rate of common Western standards.

Only in one instance has unreserved faith in Christ been discovered among the older authors. Sad to say, this was not in Gerhart Hauptmann's *Der Schuss im Park,* which is nothing but a flashily dramatized tale of far-fetched events, the story of an explorer whose African sweetheart follows him to Europe in order to take her revenge for having been deserted. One cannot help regretting that the author of *Die Weber* and of *Hanneles Himmelfahrt* has not more to say. It is, on the other hand, gratifying to see that Hermann Claudius felt no compulsion to adjust himself to the new political masters and to eliminate from his novel *Das Silberschiff* (1923), when it was republished in 1940, the vision of Christ as the lodestar, the greatest inspiration for the hapless proletarian hero of the story. The novel bears the sub-title, "The Story of Longing," and though we are not fully informed as to the yearnings of the hero, it is clear that the desire for stronger bonds of sympathy among men is one of them. The image of Christ bending compassionately over the leper will remain embedded in the mind of the hero, as it will in that of the reader, as a symbol which can bring together all those who believe in agape as the basic need of civilization.

One of the most moving confessions of Christian candour was in the subdued voice of historical pietism. Georg Schwarz wrote a brief recapitulation of the life of a Protestant minister, Johann Friedrich Flattich, who preached and demonstrated Christian virtues in the eighteenth century, *Tage und Stunden aus dem Leben eines leutseligen, gottfröhlichen Menschenfreundes, der Johann Friedrich Flattich hiess.* Simple as Flattich's days on earth were, narrow as the limits of his parish activities must appear, this man rises to a height of spirituality, worldly wisdom, and practical *savoir vivre* that cannot fail to make a great impression on all who can still hear and enjoy the voice of serene wisdom and intelligent kindness. Unorthodox as a minister, courageous in his dealings with the worldly powers that view him with suspicion, Flattich acknowledges only one essential duty, as far as his profession is concerned: to bring spiritual and material comfort to suffering people. In doing this he finds himself exalted and helped by God. "Flattich's love for his fellow-men went out from his heart in broad streams. The more he gave, the more abundantly his own inner resources replenished themselves. This occurrence is typical of higher manifestations of nature, if indeed it does not characterize the highest expression of it: the simile of a continuously replenished fountain, so often featured by the poets, is best applied to the living soul of man whose inner stores grow in the measure that he dispenses gifts." Though the events of the tale are told in a quietly flowing chronological order, the author knows how to underline where emphasis is desirable. One such occasion occurs when Flattich, pressed by his clerical friends to explain why a serene heart should be called man's most coveted possession, elaborates on common sense, tolerance, warm concern for others, peace, and blissful contact with nature as the chief ingredients of a serene mind. Again, the last scene of the book lingers in our memory as strangely eloquent for the year 1940, in which the story was published. Flattich encounters the ruling duke, the representative of a power that is "wholly of this world," as the author stresses, only to remind us: "But love comes from above." The duke, though he pays his respects to the dust-covered wanderer and states that he is eager to learn from him, spurs his horse and soon disappears in the distance, while Flattich climbs up the hill. He feels as if he were going towards heaven; "two genii standing on the gates of heaven slowly lift their trumpets, and their jubilant sounds, mingling with one another high up in the ether, sing forever the glory of a loving God who will redeem the world."

The appearance of a literary character such as Flattich, with his halo of pious thoughts and deeds, comes as a surprise: the reader is inclined to assume that the venture was possible only under the protecting garb of historical biography. Yet the same publisher (Rainer Wunderlich, Tübingen) was in 1939 responsible for the printing of a novel which features the modern counterpart of Flattich and which, if anything, speaks even more boldly of the lasting value of human kindness. The hero of *Das befreite Herz*, by Hans Löscher, does not have, to be sure, the eloquence of a trained minister such as Flattich, but in his actions he shows equal strength of conviction, depth of compassion, and perseverance. Hans Nebel, the son of poor parents, whose youth was made unhappy by a thwarted ambition to become a missionary in the Far East, sublimates his suppressed desires in a life of service and sacrifice such as few Christians nowadays dare to live. A heroic soldier and a good samaritan towards friend and foe alike in the First World War, Nebel in the years afterwards loses a small fortune through the dishonest operations of a friend whom he had wanted to help. Instead of turning bitter he devotes his meagre earnings to the support of this friend's widow, in whose home he boards without revealing his identity. It is only after his death that she finds out who he was and that his care for her extends even beyond the grave: he has left her a considerable sum which he had deposited for her with a lawyer. Nebel performs all his acts of sympathy in the most inconspicuous way, and the literary gifts of the author are equal to the task of giving life to this modern saint, without sentimentality or unctuousness. It is during a reunion of his classmates at the gymnasium that the full picture of Nebel emerges, mainly through information supplied by a doctor whose good fortune it was to cross Nebel's path time and again during the war and afterwards. The fabrics woven on Löscher's narrative loom are rich but they are also subdued in their colours. The hero is never heard to preach; the reflection of his life in the minds of his more worldly class-mates speaks with greater insistence than any direct words could do. None of these men—now doctors, lawyers, chemists—will ever forget the message implicitly contained in Nebel's life. When at the end the author is tempted to analyse piety and the good life, he does so through the voice of the lawyer who informs the widow of her windfall. "Such a light, Mrs. Peters, was our friend Nebel. Why deny the fact longer? Now that he is dead, everybody might just as well know it. He was a little man, as we unthinkingly say; but he was a great man, a pure man, one of those who possess the secret of living from within, courageously and humbly. The world is in

[165]

need of such men. . . . Men of power go through their time and carry a heavy load. The earth trembles under their feet when they pass, and their will changes the world. . . .But the humble ones, during the storm, kindle the sacred flame of humanity that glows on the hearth of eternal love. This is my belief, with which I live and with which I shall die."

There are many other signs of resistance to the attempted revaluation of all moral, religious, and humanistic values. It is well known that National Socialism drew up its own list of cardinal sins. Some of these, such as disgracing the Aryan race, or adhering to democratic principles, made the head-lines. Others were given less glaring but nevertheless dangerous publicity by literary supporters. But not all writers volunteered to lend their power of expression and vituperation to the support of the officially sanctioned table of values. Indeed, some good novelists who had undertaken to abide by the older conceptions of sin and virtue, expressed them in unmistakable terms. Willy Kramp, Edzard Schaper, and Richard Hoepner wrote tales of murder perpetrated under duress. A more robust, up-to-date conscience would not have found it difficult to send the unpleasant memory into oblivion; but not so here! The foreman of Hoepner's *Werk-meister Berthold Kramp* has killed the automobile designer who stole some of his blueprints and had for years done everything to make life miserable for him. Kramp sees no reason why he should go to the police and confess, yet he is incapable of shaking off a most bothersome feeling of guilt; his subsequent life is rendered uneasy by the struggle of subjective right and objective wrong. Finally he decides to make a clean breast of it, but collapses and dies in an office of the police building.

The presentation of the psychology of suppressed guilt, of murder which will out, is the first great distinction of this re-markable book. The second is a result of the subtle emphasis which is put on the reality of a very sensitive conscience in most human beings, a conscience that no amount of rationalization can throw out of balance for long. By way of diversity and relief the novel has an interesting set of characters and events, such as the

Kramp family, their daughter, a fine girl in spite of, or rather because of, an illegitimate child she has borne to a good-for-nothing lover whom she does not want to marry, and, most moving of all, an American automobile racer, a distinguished literary creation this, of a man who with astounding strength of mind masters his experience and his great personal affliction, a face disfigured by cancer.

No relief from the clutches of guilt is provided for in Schaper's *Der Henker*. We are throughout the story kept close to the principal character and to his inner torments. He has, as a young German-Russian officer, ordered the execution of some rebels; military prudence and the law were on his side, but not his sensitive conscience. Haunted by the spectre of a cruelty which was imposed upon him, but which perhaps could have been avoided had he but shown greater moral resistance to routine orders, he finds peace only after the relatives of some of the men he had so severely punished have forgiven him.

Reading these and other novels one thinks that they must have originated in some theocratic state, and not under National Socialism. The mood is wholly created by remorse, the thought is dominated by the awareness of man's sinful nature, and of a being much higher than a man-created God. He is, however, a merciful God; crimes committed against society can be atoned for by redoubled devotion to society. Gey, one of the main characters in Kramp's *Die Fischer von Lissau,* works off the guilt of his murder by teaching backward fishermen higher standards of living. In Hans Wörner's *König am Jykän,* Bransen, a benefactor improving the economic conditions of a remote and impoverished Norwegian valley, is finally found out to be acting as such "an incredibly good man" to compensate for the a-social operations of his days as a real-estate speculator in the United States.

Kramp, Hoepner, Schaper, and others are satisfied with their insistence on the social necessity for ethical standards such as are common to Western civilization. A number of novelists go further and try to anchor these secularized standards to a metaphysical or religious base. They may have lost the instinctive faith of Rendl

[167]

(see chapter IX) and be more cautious in their religious enthusiasm than Schwarz and Löscher, but the more or less conscious struggle for a new religious or philosophical foundation makes their work all the more significant.

Obviously some Catholic writers made use of a possible slight overlapping of National Socialism and Catholic religion, in order to hold their ground. The image of mother and child has long been used to suggest a Catholic reverence for the Holy Virgin and the Saviour child. The same image was adopted by writers of the blood and soil school to symbolize and to popularize the urge to propagation. Catholic writers seem on occasion to have relied on this possible ambiguity to confuse the watchful critics, trusting that at least some of their readers would understand and accept the religious interpretation of the image. Yet even if something of each motive is suspected, we cannot find fault, as the mother and child image both refines biological feelings and embodies religious emotions.

In *Der kleine Gott*, by Kurt Ziesel, a young peasant girl gets into trouble and decides to make an end of it all by drowning herself in the river. She walks past the church she had visited once before with her lover. The happiness of those days is gone, and gone too is her Catholic faith; the bells that peal from the tower, the image of the Holy Virgin, only serve to remind her that the religion of her childhood no longer holds any promise of help and comfort. Too proud to go back a penitent sinner, she continues through the forest to the river. She throws off her clothes and wades into the water. As the flood rises around her pregnant body, a transformation of her whole outlook on life takes place; experiencing for the first time the mystery of a new being growing in her, she forgets her suicidal intentions and a strong desire to protect the unborn child drives her back to shore, and back into life. The world all of a sudden looks sweet again, as she now sees it with the eyes of an expectant mother. The mystery of all mysteries has overpowered her. God has given her his blessing again, a new altar has risen within her, and the religious experience of former days has acquired a new and much more vital meaning.

The incident is not very convincing as a piece of psychology—why should this particular occasion suggest to the girl the significance of her condition? The symbolic intent is easily seen: a religious feeling is made to coalesce with a biological urge. For if by extolling the will to live and to bear children the author placates one master, a far greater master is also served: He who proclaimed the sanctity of all life.

The apotheosis of motherhood is repeated in a novel by Hanns Gottschalk (*Der Fremde im Dorf*). Much inferior as a work of art to Ziesel's book, it has the virtue of being less ambiguous in its purpose. The stranger who comes to the village is in all but name a saint, a genuine Christian who dares the stupid brutality of the villagers to kill him for his deeds of love and for his exhortations to tolerance. He appears with the avowed purpose of bringing back into the midst of degenerate men the God of love, a God whom he first experienced in the loving care of his own mother. This God, as the author says, is to be found in the silent growth of life, not in the boisterous ephemeral concerns of men. Of all the unexpected books of the period this is the most surprising, praising, as it does, patience, meekness, and infinite kindness even to one's worst enemies, and running parallel in the final scenes of its plot to Christ's death and resurrection.

Novels of this kind recover lost religious ground by means of emotional, if not mystic reactions. The mysteries of love and of birth are lyrically evoked to prepare a mood of wonderment and a readiness to accept supernatural influences. There is, however, another approach to religious consciousness, one which takes its start from the complementary side of cool reasoning. Strange as it may sound, Germany during the last few years witnessed a renaissance of the intellectual novel, of literary works in which at least one character, if not several, maintains a rapid fireworks of brilliant remarks and repartee. Nor is it a display of intellectual quickness for its own sake. Most often this new intellectuality has a definite aim, and the lack of religious and metaphysical imagination, so common among modern men, forms one of its chief targets.

Two novels merit special attention in this connexion, though others could be added to form a comparatively impressive list of invigorating, intellectual books: *Gullivers letzte Reise,* by Franz Wittkop, and *Der Zuschauer* by Editha Klipstein. A Gulliver novel automatically raises high expectations and places its author under a heavy obligation. This obligation is not met by Wittkop, despite a promising start. His fantastic story is of a ship's doctor landing on an island, the Isle of Mortals. The Mortals live and die at a pace which makes our average life span seem to extend into eternity. Their lives when full grown can be measured in months, but into these months they manage to crowd all ordinary human experiences: childhood, adolescence, parenthood, and old age. After a few weeks our shipwrecked doctor is talking to the grandchildren of the young people he met on his arrival. This imaginative device obviously offers a great opportunity for the observer to present the course of history, which among these islanders takes so much less time to develop than among ordinary human beings. It is mainly in this direction that the author exploits his advantage: a replica of European history passes over the stage, medieval times and the Renaissance, revolutions and counter-revolutions, government by the people and by dictators, ages that call themselves enlightened and others that live by violence and the suspension of all laws. Much to our disappointment, the only emphatic lesson extracted from this spectacle is that of the transitoriness of all things and forms. The exuberant hopes of one period are ridiculed by another; the past was not worse than the present is, and only a fool will believe that the future can bring more than illusory improvement. This may have been a bold enough reminder to make under a government which boasted of ushering in a millenium of happiness; the more lasting value of the novel is in its broadly intellectual, discursive style.

Editha Klipstein reveals in the very title of her novel, *Der Zuschauer,* that she too treats of an onlooker, a spectator who feels under no compulsion to interfere with the course of events. But though her spectator does not take much action, he is at least a fearless and independent thinker who never hesitates to state his opinions. His thought all but acquires the strength of action. A rather flimsy plot serves as the pretext for the author to stimulate discussion and to pass judgment on her time, on its loquaciousness, its unwillingness to develop more than the material possibilities of existence, and its individualism that creates no true individualities. Men have become engrossed in their desire for more power, and, since power is now measured in terms of money only, our whole civilization revolves around the formula: money and debts. The restlessness of our age and the speed of technical progress, by which the achievement of yesterday turns into the quaint museum exhibit of today, have so afflicted us that we seek incessant change and have lost the taste for static essences and the desire to be somebody.

In addition to her numerous stabs at the modern phenomenon of action without creation of anything of lasting value, Editha Klipstein also distributes a good many constructive suggestions among the characters of her novel. Man must again become conscious of his dual inheritance of natural and spiritual, biological and transcendental qualities. The first, our natural inheritance, demands of us obedience to a few basic laws which are prerequisites for peaceful society: health, love of one another, social responsibility. Though Editha Klipstein calls these natural laws, we do not fulfil them instinctively. We have to be taught their significance; and even then adherence to them is not easy. When social and political peace is secured, we must proceed to permeate natural with cultural life, in order to enjoy the serene tranquillity of wisdom and the unhurried abandon to ever present beauty, to the beauty of the moment, as the author puts it. Her insistence on a more static form of art, and of life, is worth noting. In the very style of her book, to say nothing of its content, she protests against the German craving for originality and for restlessness as something good *per se*. Things must be allowed to mature; maturity, once reached, must be enjoyed and not quickly dismissed as a mere stepping-stone to something else unless, of course, this something else is man's last and final task, a sober realization that existence is surrounded by transcendence and that things created point to a creation.

[171]

Yet there is no need, at this point, to cast off reason for mysticism. Editha Klipstein has, indeed, a great concern for a new, intellectual approach to religion. If man is to make good use of all his latent abilities, he must first of all find his true place, an expression of Pascal's she repeatedly borrows. It is reason, not emotion or enthusiasm, that should guide us in our search for higher powers. For it is intelligence, and no other faculty, that tells us of the existence of higher beings. If intelligent people had not, in our time, surrendered to unthinking youth and to the so called solutions youth is proffering, then middle-aged men would not now have become resigned to the puerile materialistic explanation of existence. Reason has to insist again on its prerogatives and to become conscious of its specific duties. One such duty is to reckon with the reality of God, to investigate it, and, once it is ascertained, to proclaim it. As things are, religion, what is left of it, has become diluted and sentimentalized, or is linked with tasks that are outside its sphere and belong to our natural functions, such as the observance of an ethical code. "God is not sentimental." But because we thought Him sentimental instead of just, good-natured instead of loving, we have come to doubt His justice and His love. The day will come when we shall find it as ridiculous to doubt the existence of God as we find it to talk about His injustice. A properly functioning reason will restore religion to its rightful place; for it was a perverted kind of logic that disproved the reality of God or of a higher life. Time and again Editha Klipstein exposes and castigates the fallacy of accepting the findings of a famished, under-developed reason, of an intellect that has not yet drawn in enough experience to pronounce on other than material aspects of life.

Der Zuschauer is easily the most intelligent novel produced during the anti-intellectual interregnum, and in the absence, from Germany, of Thomas Mann. We may of course regret that Editha Klipstein has made no attempt (if we disregard the symbolic burning down of an old castle) to show her findings translated into actions of everyday life. For while the plot is strong enough to give flesh and blood to its many characters, and to erase all impression of their being ideological puppets only, it does not actually rebuild the world in which it is set. To expect such direct action may be asking too much at a time when emphasis on intellectual integrity, scorn for the activism of greenhorns, and belief in other than physical realities were themselves acts of bold defiance of official trends.

"He who does not know the world is not mature enough to know heaven," Editha Klipstein says. The statement is a clear indication of the kind of reason with which she re-defines the essence of religion. It is a reason that starts from the intelligently analysed reality of existence, from the needs of men and from their hopes and disappointments. It is not, for instance, a reason that is nourished on dogmatic issues and traditions.

Such is the evidence that has been found of the survival of the Western tradition, which in its broadest sense rests on the co-ordination of humanitarian emotions with sound reason, in order to promote the welfare of all people, to guarantee their freedom, and to encourage their spiritual aspirations. Mr. Schütz in *Pens under the Swastika* (1946) emphatically states that there is enough of the Western substance left in Germany to initiate movements in the direction of a new humanism, Christian or secular. Whether such additional information as will gradually come to light is going to strengthen or damp our hopes, remains to be seen. Meanwhile it is well to remember that in part we shall find what we are looking for. *Comment pourrais-je chercher, si je n'avais pas déjà trouvé?* Our own attitude, hopeful or distrustful, if it cannot alter what the past has done, will at any rate influence the character of the German literature of tomorrow.

Bibliography

AHLERS, RUDOLF. Das weite Land. 1940.
ALTEN, ELLIDA VON. Kindersommer. 1941.
ANDERL, RUDOLF. Haus in der Sonne. 1942.
ANDREAE, ILLA. Der griechische Traum. 1943.
ANDREEVSKY, ALEXANDER VON. Der Weg zum Gral. 1941.
ANSCHÜTZ, ALBERT. Hochzeit in Innsbruck. 1942.
ATTENBERGER, TONI. Der endlose Wald. 1940.
BAGIER, GUIDO. Das tönende Licht. 1943.
BARKHAUSEN, JOACHIM. Ohm Krüger. 1941.
BARTH, EMIL. Das Lorbeerufer. 1942.
BARTHEL, MAX. Das Land auf den Bergen. 1939.
BARTZ, KARL. Lilienbanner und Preussenaar. 1940.
BASSOE-HEJKEN. Fischer von Erlach. 1942.
BAUER, HEINRICH. Michelangelo. 1944.
BAUER, JOSEF MARTIN. Das Herz. 1940.
————Das Mädchen auf Stachet. 1940.
BAUMGARTEN, HANS. Moritz von Sachsen. 1942.
BECHEM, ANNEMARIE. Drache im Gelderland. 1943.
BECKER, O. E. H. Das australische Abenteuer. 1939.
BEHREND, DORA ELEONORE. Rose aus dem Werder. 1942.
————Spätsonne. 1942.
BEIELSTEIN, FELIX WILHELM. Der grosse Imhoff. 1939.
BEITL, RICHARD. Angelika. 1941.
BELZNER, EMIL. Ich bin der König. 1940.
BENRATH, HENRY. Die Kaiserin Theophano. 1940.

See also last paragraph of the Preface.

Owing to a not infrequent practice among German writers of changing publishers after 1932 and of reissuing books without indicating the year of their first appearance, complete bibliographical accuracy is difficult to achieve.

The books listed here are available in the Library of the University of Toronto.

BENTLAGE, MARGARETE ZUR. Geheimnis im Hunebrook. 1943.
BERENS-TOTENOHL, JOSEFA. Der Fels. 1943.
BERGENGRUEN, WERNER. Am Himmel wie auf Erden. 1940.
———Herzog Karl der Kühne. 1943.
BERGLAR-SCHROER, PAUL. Der feuerspeiende Berg. 1943.
BERKUN, ARTHUR. Kamerad Bursche. 1942.
BERTOLOLY, PAUL. Dora Holdenrieth. 1939.
BESTE, KONRAD. Das Land der Zwerge. 1939.
BETSCH, ROLAND. Ballade am Strom. 1939.
BETZNER, ANTON. Basalt. 1942.
BEYERLEIN, FRANZ ADAM. Johanna Rosina. 1942.
BLUNCK, HANS FRIEDRICH. Die Jägerin. 1940.
BOGER, MARGOT. Die goldene Maske. 1943.
BÖHM-LEMKE, WALTER. Zwei unter Millionen. 1940.
BORIS, OTTO. Die Fischerinsel. 1942.
———Der Grenzbauer. 1943.
BORNEMANN, HANNS. Der auf Tornhagen. 1941.
BÖTTCHER, MAXIMILIAN. Krach im Vorderhaus. 1940.
———Die Wolfrechts. 1940.
BRAACH, JOHANNES HEINRICH. Quilepp und Quila. 1941.
BRAUTLACHT, ERICH. Meister Schure. 1941.
BREHM, BRUNO. Auf Wiedersehn, Susanne! 1939.
———Die sanfte Gewalt. 1940.
———Ein Schloss in Böhmen. 1944.
BRIEGER, ALFRED. Sehnsucht. 1944.
BRINCKEN, GERTRUD VON DEN. Unsterbliche Wälder. 1941.
BRINKMANN, OTTO. Verwirrung um Irene. 1942.
BRITZEN, ANGELA VON. Wir haben dich gemeint. 1940.
BROEHL-DELHAES, CHRISTEL. Worte, die der Mund nicht
    sprach . . .! 1940.
BRÖKER, HEINZ. Die tapferen Tage. 1944.
BRUNNGRABER, RUDOLF. Opiumkrieg. 1939.
———Zucker aus Cuba. 1941.
BRUNS, MARIANNE. Das rechtschaffene Herz. 1939.
BRUSTGI, FRANZ GEORG. Eustachius Holderkling. 1939.
BUGGE, GÜNTHER. Der Alchimist. 1941.
BUNTZEL, IRMA. Als ich aufsah war ich allein. 1943.
BÜRKLE, VEIT. Lasst das Frühjahr kommen. 1940.
BURRE, PAUL. Es reiten die wilden Jäger. 1940.

BUSSE, HERMANN ERIS. Der Erdgeist. 1939.

———Girlegig. 1941.

CALOW, RICHARD. Die Junker von Wefelow. 1941.

CAROSSA, HANS. Das Jahr der schönen Täuschungen. 1941.

CHRISTOPH, FRANK E. Die Hazienda. 1940.

———Sehnsucht nach der Heimat. 1943.

COELLEN, GRETE. Wilma zwischen den Müttern. 1943.

DAHMEN, WALTHER. Mitte des Lebens. 1941.

DAUMANN, RUDOLF HEINRICH. Patrouille gegen den Tod. 1939.

DIEHL, LUDWIG. Der Meister und die Mütter. 1941.

DIESEL, EUGEN. Autoreise 1905. 1941.

DIETZ, FRANZ. Die Gesellschaft der Jugend. 1939.

DILL, LIESBET. Liebe. 1939.

DITTMER, HANS. Annenhof. 1939.

DODERER, HEIMITO VON. Ein Umweg. 1940.

DÜRING, THEKLA VON. Caroline. 1942.

EBERMAYER, ERICH. Unter anderm Himmel. 1942.

ECKMANN, HEINRICH. Das blühende Leben. 1939.

EGGERS, KURT. Der Tanz aus der Reihe. 1939.

EICHTHAL, RUDOLF VON. Die goldene Spange. 1941.

ELBERTZHAGEN, TH. W. Die Brückensymphonie. 1941.

ELBWART, WILM VON. Ein Mensch, ein Berg, Gewalten. 1941.

ELERT, GEORG. Gastspiel in Chiriqui. 1944.

ELLERT, GERHART. Michelangelo. 1942.

ENGELKES, GUSTAV G. Sturmflut. 1943.

ENGSTLER, OTTO HANS. Das Leben des Hartwig Brückner. 1943.

EURINGER, RICHARD. Der Serasker. 1939.

EWERBECK, BETINA. Angela Koldewey. 1939.

EWERS, HANS. Kilian Menkes Veränderung. 1941.

FALKENSTERN, ANNA MARIA. Zwischen den Mächten. 1941.

FALLADA, HANS. Damals bei uns daheim. 1941.

———Heute bei uns zu Haus. 1943.

FECHTER, PAUL. Der Herr Ober. 1940.

FINCKENSTEIN, OTTFRIED GRAF. Dämmerung. 1942.

FRANCÉ-HARRAR, A. Und eines Tages. 1940.

FRANCHY, FRANZ K. Maurus und sein Turm. 1941.

FRANK, ERNST. Das beschriebene Schwert. 1943.

FREUMBICHLER, JOHANNES. Auszug und Heimkehr des Jodok Fink. 1942.

FRIEDRICH, HANS. Der gekrönte Kaufmann. 1944.

FROMME-BECHEM, ANNEMARIE. Die grosse Ordnung. 1943.

FUNDER, C. TRONIER. Die grosse Fuhre. 1943.

FUSSENEGGER, GERTRUD. Die Leute auf Falbeson. 1940.

GABELE, ANTON. In einem kühlen Grunde. 1939.

GANTER, CHRISTOPH ERIK. Panama. 1942.

GEHLEN, ENGELBERT. Himmelblaue Segel. 1943.

GEISSLER, HORST WOLFRAM. Menuett im Park. 1940.

GERVES, GEORG. Schwarze Marga. 1942.

GIERER, BERCHTOLD. Pallasch und Federkiel. 1939.

————Geschlechter am See. 1940.

GIRARDI, ANTON MARIA. Das Schicksal setzt den Hobel an. 1941.

GLUTH, OSKAR. Pan im Schilf. 1940.

GOEDECKE, RENATE. Die Brigg Selmar Fernando. 1941.

GÖSSL, FRANZ. Der verschenkte Hof. 1942.

GOTHE, OTTO. Sumpferz. 1941.

GOTTSCHALK, HANNS. Der Fremde im Dorf. 1940.

GRABENHORST, GEORG. Die Reise nach Luzern. 1939.

GRAU, ERNST. Vor dem letzten Akt. 1944.

GRAUTOFF, ERNA. Herrscher über Traum und Leben. 1940.

GRIESE, FRIEDRICH. Die Weissköpfe. 1939.

GRIX, ARTHUR E. Umweg über Frisco. 1943.

GRUBER, GISI. Ein allzu schwarzes Schäflein. 1941.

GRUELICH, A. T. Freundschaft um Barbara. 1941.

GÜNTHER, JOHANNES. Sturz der Maske. 1943.

GURK, PAUL. Iskander. 1944.

GUTTING, WILLI. Die Aalfischer. 1943.

HABECK, FRITZ. Der Scholar vom linken Galgen. 1941.

HAJEK, EGON. Meister Johannes. 1942.

HARDER, HANS. Klim. 1940.

HARMS, WILLI. Der neue Bürgermeister. 1942.

HARNISCH, JOHANNES W. Der kleine Prinz. 1940.

HARTMANN, HEINZ. Das Erbe von Liebenstein. 1941.

HARTMANN, WOLF JUSTIN. Mann im Mars. 1940.

HAUPTMANN, GERHART. Der Schuss im Park. 1941.

HAYDUK, ALFONS. Sturm über Schlesien. 1940.

HEIN, ALFRED. Du selber bist Musik. 1942.

HEINE, GERHARD. Der Mann, der nach Syrakus spazieren ging. 1940.

HEINRICH, EDITH. Der Leuchtturm. 1943.

[177]

HEITMANN, HANS. Die Flut. 1942.

HELWIG, WERNER. Raubfischer in Hellas. 1939.

———Im Dickicht des Pelion. 1942.

HENZ, RUDOLF. Der Kurier des Kaisers. 1941.

———Der grosse Sturm. 1943.

HERGENBRECHT, PETER. Vorabend. 1939.

HERSE, HENRIK. Die Schlacht der weissen Schiffe. 1939.

———Wahr dich Garde, der Bauer kommt! 1939.

———Reiter für Deutsch-Südwest. 1941.

———Zur Raa fuhr auf ein roter Schild. 1943.

HEYCK, HANS. Der grosse König. 1940.

HEYNICKE, KURT. Der Baum, der in den Himmel wächst. 1940.

———Rosen blühen auch im Herbst. 1942.

HÖCHSTETTER, SOPHIE. Im Tauwind. 1941.

HÖCKER, PAUL OSKAR. Ich liebe Dich. 1940.

HOEHNE, EDMUND. Die Rache durch Gulliver. 1941.

HOLLANDER, WALTHER VON. Therese Larotta. 1939.

———Akazien. 1941.

HOLLENBACH, HANS-HEINRICH. Die trotzige Stadt. 1942.

HOLZACH, HANS. Der goldene Rahmen. 1939.

HOEPNER, RICHARD. Werkmeister Berthold Kramp. 1939.

HOPPE, MAREI J. Der im weissen Turban. 1942.

HOERNER, HERBERT VON. Der graue Reiter. 1940.

HUCH, FELIX. Mozart. 1941.

IHLE, HANS. Der Jagdteufel. 1941.

ISEMANN, BERND. Das härtere Eisen. 1942.

———Die Ameisenstadt. 1943.

JACOBI, HEINRICH. Der Grossmast. 1943.

JANECKE, ROBERT. Friedrich und Sophie. 1940.

JELUSICH, MIRKO. Der Soldat. 1939.

———Der Traum vom Reich. 1941.

JOHANN, A. E. Der Tod im Busch. 1940.

———Das Land ohne Herz. 1942.

———Im Strom. 1943.

JUNG, ELSE. Die Jensensippe. 1942.

JÜNGER, ERNST. Auf den Marmorklippen. 1939.

JUNGHERR, VICTOR GEORG. Der Weg der Skaringa. 1940.

KADEN, HERMANN WALTER. Das Haus zu den vier Winden. 1943.

KAEMPFFER, ADOLF. Ritt gen Mitternacht. 1939.

KAPPUS, FRANZ XAVIER. Flammende Schatten. 1944.
KARRASCH, ALFRED. Kopernikus. 1944.
KEPPELMÜLLER, BERTOLD. Das Gesetz der Sterne. 1942.
KERNMAYR, HANS GUSTL. Die grosse Wanderung. 1939.
KESSLER, WALTHER. Und eines Tages öffnet sich die Tür. 1941.
KIRN, RICHARD. Das grosse Spiel. 1942.
KITZINGER, HANS. Die Farm am Erongo. 1940.
KLASS, GERT VON. Die Liebe des Leutnants Wartenstein. 1940.
KLEIN, FRITZ. Smaragde unter dem Urwald. 1941.
KLIPSTEIN, EDITHA. Der Zuschauer. 1942.
KLUGE, KURT. Die Zaubergeige. 1940.
KNOBLOCH, HILDE. Der Feuergeist. 1941.
KNYPHAUSEN, ANTON GRAF. Sebastian am Seitenweg. 1939.
KOBER, A. H. Zirkus Renz. 1943.
KÖHLER, THEODOR HEINZ. Der junge Daniel. 1940.
KOHLHAAS, WILHELM. Mars und Skorpion. 1939.
KRAFT, ZDENKO VON. Alexanderzug. 1940.
KRAMER, WALTER. Gestaute Flut. 1941.
KRAMP, WILLY. Die Fischer von Lissau. 1939.
————Die Jünglinge. 1943.
KRIEGER-WIMPF, JOHANNA. Sommerliche Begegnung. 1943.
KRIES, GERDA VON. Weichselwinde. 1942.
KUBIE, WILHELM. Professor Frauenschuh. 1939.
KÜNKEL, HANS. Ein Arzt sucht seinen Weg. 1939.
————Laszlo. 1941.
KUNZEMANN, GERTRUD. Wiedergeboren. 1942.
KÜPER, JOSEF. Das Dukatenmännchen. 1941.
KURZ, KARL FRIEDRICH. Herrn Erlings Magd. 1943.
LAMBERT, KÄTHE. Das fremde Mädchen Julia. 1942.
LANDESEN, WERA VON. Die rote Kerze. 1942.
LANDGRAF, ARTUR. Hieselstal. 1941.
LANGERMANN, J. CHR. F. VON. Schaff Gold, Böttger! 1942.
LANGEWIESCHE, MARIANNE. Königin der Meere. 1940.
————Die Allerheiligen Bucht. 1942.
LEHR, HANS. Die Freiwilligen vom grossen Wasser. 1941.
LEIP, HANS. Das Muschelhorn. 1940.
————Jan Himp und die kleine Brise. 1941.
————Der Gast. 1943.
LEITICH, ANN TIZIA. Amor im Wappen. 1940.

LETTENMAIR, J. G. Mirko und Alke. 1942.

LEUTERITZ, GUSTAV. Die Königsbotschaft. 1940.

LINDEMANN, FRIEDRICH. Sohn seiner Firma. 1939.

LOBSIEN, WILHELM. Segnende Erde. 1942.

LÖHNDORFF, ERNST F. Khaiberpass. 1941.

LORENZ, ALBERT. Unter Gottes Gewittern. 1943.

LORENZ, GERHARD. Unrast. 1943.

LOREY, HEINZ. Rubens. 1943.

LOERKE, GEORG. Das Spiel mit dem Feuer. 1941.

LÖSCHER, HANS. Das befreite Herz. 1939.

LÖW, RUDOLF. Achilles Kern. 1943.

LÜHE, VERONIKA. Henner von Plauen. 1943.

LUSERKE, MARTIN. Wikinger: Die hohe See. 1941.

MAGG, FRANZ JOSEPH. Arzt sein. 1942.

MANNS, BENNO LUDWIG. Die Chronik vom köstlichen Leben. 1942.

————Schwalben über Lippoldsburg. 1943.

MARTI, ERNST OTTO. Balduin Ritters Heimkehr. 1942.

MATHAR, LUDWIG. Der Reichsfeldmarschall. 1939.

MATTHAEI, LOTHAR. Irgendwo drüben in Kanada. 1942.

MAYER, ANTON. Der Zug der bunten Masken. 1940.

MAYER, ERICH AUGUST. Der Knecht. 1943.

MELCHERS, MARIA. Der lange Becker. 1941.

MENZEL, HERYBERT. Das Siebengestirn. 1943.

MERKER, EMIL. Die wilden Geheimnisse. 1943.

METTENLEITER, FRITZ. Nikolaus Kopernikus. 1943.

MICHAEL, FRIEDRICH. Silvia und die Freier. 1941.

MICHAEL, RUDOLF. Roman einer Weltreise. 1940.

MICHELS, JOSEF. Flammen im Emscherbruch. 1942.

MIKELEITIS, EDITH. Das ewige Bildnis. 1942.

MITTERER, ERIKA. Der Fürst der Welt. 1940.

MÖLLER, KARL VON. Der Savoyer. 1939.

————Das steinerne Schachbrett. 1941.

MOLZAHN, ILSE. Töchter der Erde. 1941.

MÜLLER-GÖGLER, MARIA. Beatrix von Schwaben. 1942.

MUMELTER, HUBERT. Schatten im Schnee. 1942.

MUNGENAST, E. M. Der Pedant. 1939.

————Der Zauberer Muzot. 1939.

NEBE, BORIS. Juans Söhne. 1943.

NELISSEN-HAKEN, BRUNO. Die Tümpelbrüder. 1943.

NEUDORFER, RICHARD. Jürg Engelprecht. 1942.

NEURATH, KARL. Einsame Frauen. 1942.

NEUSTÄDTER, ERWIN. Mohn im Ährenfeld. 1943.

NICKOL, HANNS. Die wachsende Schuld. 1941.

NIDDA, ROLAND KRUG VON. Französische Elegie. 1941.

NÖLLE, FRITZ. Die gläserne Wand. 1940.

———Herrn Kesperleins seltsame Reise. 1942.

NORFOLK, FRIEDRICH. Der Kondottiere. 1939.

———Herz im Panzer. 1942.

NOWAK, HANS. Wenn es Tag wird. 1942.

OBERKOFLER, JOSEF GEORG. Der Bannwald. 1939.

———Die Flachsbraut. 1942.

OELLERS, WERNER. Die neuen Augen. 1940.

———Das beharrliche Leben. 1942.

ORTNER, EUGEN. Das Weltreich der Fugger. 1941.

———Georg Friedrich Händel. 1942.

———Glück und Macht der Fugger. 1943.

OSTEN, MARISSA VON DER. Petja. 1941.

OTTOW, FRED. Die Brautfahrt nach Petersburg. 1943.

PASTENACI, KURT. Herzog Bojo. 1939.

———Der Herzog und die Könige. 1942.

PAUST, OTTO. Menschen unterm Hammer. 1942.

PEGEL, WALTER. Die fernen Nächte. 1939.

PELLON, ALFRED. Gozell Garin. 1942.

PETERNELL, PERT. Der König der Ärzte. 1941.

PEUCKERT, WILL-ERICH. Nikolaus Kopernikus. 1943.

PFLEGHAR, ARTUR JOST. Die Islandreiter. 1939.

PIDOLL, CARL VON. Boemo Divino. 1943.

PLEYER, WILHELM. Tal der Kindheit. 1940.

POHL, GERHART. Der verrückte Ferdinand. 1939.

PORTEN, NELLIE. Ein Stück Wegs mit Monika. 1943.

PRILL, VERA. Klingsors Schloss. 1941.

PÜLTZ, WILHELM. Unter dem Machangelbaum. 1941.

QUINDT, WILLIAM. Die Strasse der Elefanten. 1939.

———Bambino. 1940.

———Der weisse Wolf. 1941.

RABL, HANS. Der Strom zieht nach West. 1941.

RAFFAY, R. M. Ban Michael. 1941.

RAINALTER, ERWIN H. Mirabell. 1942.

RAKETTE, EGON. H. Planwagen. 1940.
RAMLOW, RUDOLF. Die letzte Freistatt. 1940.
————Albrecht der Bär. 1942.
RATHJE, ARTHUR. Weisse und schwarze Erde. 1943.
RENDL, GEORG. Ein fröhlicher Mensch. 1942.
REYHING, HANS. Der Klausenhof. 1942.
————Der tausendjährige Acker. 1942.
RINGELING, GERHARD. Karges Land. 1939.
RITTER-ELSASS, LINA. Martin Schongauer. 1942.
ROCH, HERBERT, Solange das Herz schlägt. 1943.
RÖCKEN, KURT WALTER. Die Damen in der Glöckchenstube. 1940.
ROMBACH, OTTO. Der junge Herr Alexius. 1940.
ROTHE, CARL. Olivia. 1940.
RUMMEL, CARL JOHANNES. Kaiser, Gott und Reich. 1941.
RÜTTERS, HUGO. Das flandrische Konzert. 1942.
SANDER, ULRICH. Sturm in der Düne. 1942.
————Die Kinderfamilie. 1943.
SASSMANN, HANS. Xanthippe. 1944.
SCHAPER, EDZARD. Der Henker. 1943.
SCHELLER, THILO. Klaus Störtebeker. 1942.
SCHENK, GUSTAV. Das wunderbare Leben. 1943.
SCHENZINGER, KARL ALOYS. Metall. 1939.
SCHIEL, CAROLA. Stern und Erde. 1943.
SCHILLING, HEINAR. Ein aufrechter Mann. 1944.
SCHIMMEL-FALKENAU, WALTER. Die wandernde Madonna.
SCHLAGINTWEIT, FELIX. Ein verliebtes Leben. 1943.
SCHMIDT-PRETORIA, WERNER. Ein Präsident. 1942.
SCHMÜCKLE, GEORG HEINRICH. König und Kaiser. 1942.
SCHNABEL, ERNST. Nachtwind. 1942.
SCHNEIDER, MARIA. Dichter, Tod und Liebe. 1941.
————Konradin. 1942.
SCHNEIDER-SCHELDE, RUDOLF. Offenes Fenster. 1944.
SCHOLZ, HUGO. Die weisse Wolke. 1942.
SCHÖNHOLTZ, ERNST HOFMANN VON. Wiederaufnahme Fall Lerna.
  1942.
SCHREIBER, ILSE. Die Flucht ins Paradies. 1939.
SCHREYER, LOTHAR. Der Untergang von Byzanz. 1942.
SCHREYVOGEL, FRIEDRICH. Grillparzer. 1940.
————Die Nibelungen. 1941.
————Eine Schicksalssymphonie. 1941.

SCHRÖER, GUSTAV. Die Lawine von St. Thomas. 1939.
————Die Wiedes. 1940.
SCHULENBURG, WERNER VON DER. Stechinelli. 1942.
SCHULTZE-KUNSTMANN, LISA. Die Junggesellen von Annenthal. 1941.
SCHULZ, KURD. Michael Conrad. 1942.
SCHUPP, JOHANNES MARTIN. Hans Undög. 1943.
SCHWARZ, GEORG. Tage und Stunden aus dem Leben eines leutseligen, gottfröhlichen Menschenfreundes, der Johann Friedrich Flattich hiess. 1940.
SCHWARZKOPF, NIKOLAUS. Der Feldhäfner. 1941.
————Der schwarze Nikolaus. 1944.
SEELHOFF, PAUL. Bauern und Möwen. 1941.
————Acker und Steine. 1943.
SEIDEL, INA. Unser Freund Peregrin. 1940.
SEXAU, RICHARD. Märztrieb. 1941.
SIEG, PAUL EUGEN. Detatom. 1944.
SIMPSON, WILLIAM VON. Der Enkel. 1939.
SLEZAK, LEO. Rückfall. 1940.
SNELL, HERTA. Abenteuer in Kyparissia. 1941.
SOEDING, ELLEN. Das Höfchen. 1939.
SPERLING, WALTER. Wassernächte. 1941.
SPIESSER, FRITZ. Westliche Robinsonade. 1940.
SPOERL, HEINRICH. Der Gasmann, 1940.
SPRIEGEL, ANNALIESE. Das innere Bild. 1942.
STACHELS, JOSEF. Der Sommer fährt dahin. 1943.
STAHL, HERMANN. Die Orgel der Wälder. 1939.
————Die Heimkehr des Odysseus. 1940.
————Langsam steigt die Flut. 1943.
STANIETZ, WALTHER. Das tägliche Brot. 1940.
STEHR, DIETRICH. Eusebius und die Furchtsamen. 1942.
STEHR, HERMANN. Damian. 1944.
STEINBERG, WERNER. Das Antlitz Daniels. 1942.
STEINMANN, HERBERT. Der Kurier des Königs. 1939.
STENBOCK-FERMOR, GRAF ALEXANDER. Schloss Teerkuhlen. 1942.
STEUBER, WERNER. Arzt und Soldat in drei Erdteilen. 1940.
STRAUSS, EMIL. Lebenstanz. 1940.
STRAUSS UND TORNEY, LULU VON. Der jüngste Tag. 1940.
STRENGER, HERMANN. Strom aus der Erde. 1942.
STRESAU, HERMANN. Adler über Gallien. 1942.

STROHMEYER, CURT. Mein silbergrauer Weggefährte. 1943.
STÜHLEN, PETER. Das Erbe. 1941.
STURM, STEFAN. Wildengrund. 1942.
TIMMERMANNS, RUDOLF. Aufzeichnungen, Flug und Tod des Geo
    Chavez. 1940.
TOISY, GEORGHEINRICH. Das Dorf ruft. 1941.
TRENCK, SIEGFRIED VON DER. Reichardt aus der Fülle. 1941.
TRENKER, LUIS. Hauptmann Ladurner. 1940.
TRÜSTEDT, HARO. Schänke Gott und Saitenspiel. 1940.
TÜGEL, LUDWIG. Die Freundschaft. 1939.
TÜGEL, TETJUS. Gold im Nebel. 1943.
UDEN, HORST. Gold und Reiherfedern. 1941.
———Der Unsterblichkeits-Konzern. 1943.
UHDE, SOFIE VON. Sommer in Haus Ulmenhöh. 1940.
ULLRICH, HANS. Der Hexenpastor. 1939.
UNGER, HELLMUTH. Sendung und Gewissen. 1941.
VATER, FRITZ. Herr Heinrich. 1941.
VELTER, JOSEPH M. Unruhig ist unser Herz. 1942.
VENATIER, HANS. Vogt Bartold. 1943.
VOGT, HELMUT. Oberst Hagenachs Gäste. 1941.
———Der Königstraum. 1943.
VOLCK, ERNA. Die Kerzeninsel. 1939.
VOLLMER, WALTER. Die Pöttersleute. 1940.
VRING, GEORG VON DER. Der Büchsenspanner des Herzogs. 1944.
WALDE, HILDE. Die andere Maria. 1940.
WALTER, ROBERT. Michel Unverloren. 1940.
WALZ, WERNER. Das tolle Jahr. 1943.
WATZLIK, HANS. Die Leturner Hütte. 1942.
———Die Krönungsoper. 1944.
WEBER, FRITZ. Der zerrissene Himmel. 1943.
WEHNER, JOSEF MAGNUS. Erste Liebe. 1941.
WEIGAND, WILHELM. Der Ruf am Morgen. 1941.
WEINBERG, JOSEF. Der rote und der schwarze Utz. 1943.
WELK, EHM. Die Gerechten von Kummerow. 1943.
WENDT, ELL. Sommergäste in Sophienlust. 1939.
———Wir plus drei. 1940.
———Die stolze Nymphe. 1942.
WENDT, HERBERT. Der Forst der sieben Hügel. 1941.
WENTER, JOSEF. Leise, leise! liebe Quelle. 1941.

WERLBERGER, HANS. Wolkentanz. 1941.

WESTKIRCH, LUISE. Der Hof im Moor. 1941.

WIEN, ALFRED. Um Menschen und Mächte. 1942.

WIESSALLA, JOSEF. Der Orpheusbecher. 1942.

WILHELM, HANS HERMANN. Die Wege der Brackenhoffs. 1939.

————Robert Wandelt. 1944.

WILUTZKY, ELSA. Die heilige Nacht der Gonschorras. 1941.

————Der Preusse Birkandt. 1943.

WINNIG, AUGUST. Das Buch Wanderschaft. 1941.

WINTER, SIEGFRIED MARTIN. Südamerikanische Wanderjahre. 1941.

WIRBITZKY, WILHELM. In zwei Welten. 1943.

WITTKOP, JUSTUS FRANZ. Gullivers letzte Reise. 1941.

WÖRNER, HANS. König am Jykän. 1940.

————Flugschüler Ungenat. 1941.

————Der Weg durch die Stadt. 1943.

WURM, ERNST. Der Bürger. 1941.

————Yüan Schi-Kai. 1942.

ZEDTWITZ, FRANZ GRAF. Der Untergang des Sonnenreiches. 1939.

————Feldmünster. 1940.

ZERKAULEN, HEINRICH. Narren von gestern, Helden von heute. 1941.

ZICKEL, REINHOLD. Strom. 1940.

ZIERMAIR, JOSEF. Der Bruckhof. 1941.

————Feindschaft auf der Gramai. 1943.

ZIESEL, KURT. Der kleine Gott. 1939.

————Verwandlung der Herzen. 1941.

ZORN, MICHAEL. Schicksal um den Immhof. 1941.

Index of Authors

Lightning Source UK Ltd.
Milton Keynes UK
UKOW04f0631111017

310762UK00001B/19/P